Giraffe

Animal
Series editor: Jonathan Burt

Already published

Crow
Boria Sax

Ant
Charlotte Sleigh

Tortoise
Peter Young

Cockroach
Marion Copeland

Dog
Susan McHugh

Oyster
Rebecca Stott

Bear
Robert E. Bieder

Bee
Claire Preston

Rat
Jonathan Burt

Snake
Drake Stutesman

Falcon
Helen Macdonald

Whale
Joe Roman

Parrot
Paul Carter

Tiger
Susie Green

Salmon
Peter Coates

Fox
Martin Wallen

Fly
Steven Connor

Cat
Katharine M. Rogers

Peacock
Christine E. Jackson

Cow
Hannah Velten

Swan
Peter Young

Shark
Dean Crawford

Duck
Victoria de Rijke

Rhinoceros
Kelly Enright

Horse
Elaine Walker

Moose
Kevin Jackson

Elephant
Dan Wylie

Eel
Richard Schweid

Ape
John Sorenson

Penguin
Stephen Martin

Owl
Desmond Morris

Pigeon
Barbara Allen

Snail
Peter Williams

Hare
Simon Carnell

Lion
Deirdre Jackson

Camel
Robert Irwin

Otter
Daniel Allen

Spider
Katarzyna & Sergiusz
Michalski

Giraffe

Edgar Williams

REAKTION BOOKS

Published by
REAKTION BOOKS LTD
33 Great Sutton Street
London EC1V 0DX, UK
www.reaktionbooks.co.uk

First published 2010

Printed and bound in China by C&C Offset Printing Co., Ltd

British Library Cataloguing in Publication Data
Williams, Edgar
    Giraffe. – (Animal)
    1. Giraffe 2. Giraffe in art.
    3. Giraffe in literature.
    4. Human-animal relationships – History.
    I. Title
    599.6'38-DC22

ISBN: 978 1 86189 764 0

Contents

1 The Global Giraffe 7
2 The Giraffe Inside and Out 21
3 The Ancient Giraffe from the Stone Age
  to Victoria 45
4 The Giraffe Returns to Europe 72
5 The Modern Giraffe 101
6 The Cultural Giraffe 116

Timeline of the Giraffe 152
References 154
Select Bibliography 163
Associations and Websites 165
Acknowledgements 167
Photo Acknowledgements 168
Index 170

1 The Global Giraffe

The giraffe is instantly recognizable, with its tall neck, strange angular head, long knobbly legs, golden-brown mottled coat and long, swishing tail. Everything about a giraffe is big or unusual and consequently the giraffe has fascinated man throughout its history, with its quiet and lofty stance representing in the human psyche virtue, peace and harmony.

Many thousands of years ago, the giraffe and its ancestors were common throughout the whole of Africa, Southern Europe and India. Sadly, this is no longer so and now it is found only in Africa. The giraffe and its close relative the okapi are now the only living representatives of the Giraffidae family.

The giraffe, once common throughout Africa, has seen its range continuously shrink. In the past eight hundred years or so the Northern giraffe has disappeared from North Africa as creeping desertification removed the necessary vegetation. Even today, the giraffe's range is continually threatened. The western populations (Western or Nigerian giraffe) are most acutely affected, with only a few hundred individuals now remaining in the wild. The only substantial populations left are in east and southern Africa, protected in the many national parks.

The origin of the modern giraffe is unclear, as the fossil history of the Giraffidae is incomplete. This lack of a clear ancestral path allows for vigorous scientific and philosophical debate and

An artist's impression of *Sivatherium*, an extinct cousin of the giraffe. This Pleistocene giraffe lacks a long neck but has the two extra horns on its forehead.

continues to engender controversial literary sparring between evolutionists and non-evolutionists, such as the advocates of intelligent design and creationism. The reason for this controversy is that the known fossil record does not explain how the giraffe got its long neck. All the fossil ancestors discovered so far have relatively short necks, like the giraffe's only extant cousin, the okapi, so how, where and when did the neck suddenly elongate or evolve? Or was it formed by some as yet undiscovered mechanism unexplained by the theory of evolution?

The giraffe is a two or even-toed ruminant and shares some common ancestry and therefore physiology with cows (Bovidae), deers (Cervidae) and camels (Camelus). The so-called Giraffidae family tree starts some 25 million years ago with an antelope-type animal called the Teruelia, named after the location in which the fossils were found, the Teruel Basin in Spain.[1] Before the Teruelia became extinct two subfamilies arose, the Climaco-ceratidae and the Canthumerycidae. The latter led to the recently extinct Sivatherium species. These massive ox-like beasts were widespread across Africa, Europe and western Asia. The first fossil bones were first discovered in the Silwalik Hills of India in 1827, by Lieutenants Baker and Durand of the British army.[2] Sivatherium (meaning 'wild beast of Shiva' – the Hindu lord of spirits and protector of cattle) had a short neck, long front legs, and large palmate horns like those of the modern moose or elk, but unlike a deer it had two small conical horns above the eyes, similar to the ossicones seen above the eyes of the modern-day giraffe. The palmate horns were most probably made of bony plates covered in skin like those of the modern-day deer and not the hollow skin-free horn found in cows. This Pleistocene giraffe was probably extant and roaming around India and the Middle East until relatively recently, as there is tentative evidence that they were known by the Sumerians six thousand years ago, who at this time had begun to domesticate the horse and ass.[3] This evidence came from an archaeological dig in the 1930s in Kish, Iraq, where a copper rein ring from a chariot dated to 3500 BC was uncovered. Mounted on this ring is what looks like at first sight a stag tethered by a rope, but what is unusual is that the animal has two horns above the eyes, and on close examination looks more like the Sivatherium than any known species of deer. If still alive today it might have been further domesticated, like its relative the cow.

It is the Canthumerycids that gave rise to the present day giraffe and okapi. Early fossils (twenty million years old) found in Africa, such as *Canthumeryx sirtense*, show a small antelope-like creature. Next, the *Giraffokeryx* (sixteen million years ago) appeared, which had distinct ossicones and a giraffine skull of around fifty centimetres in length.[4] Then, ten million years

A Bushman cave
painting of two
giraffes, Nswatugi,
Zimbabwe.

ago, when the climate and the distribution of land masses was
different from today, there was a rapid divergence of new giraffe
species; fossil remains have been found all around the Mediterranean, throughout Africa, the Middle East, India and as far
afield as Mongolia.[5] Eventually the Asian, Indian and European
Giraffidae became extinct (about four million years ago) and
only the African giraffes were left.

The final African lineage contained five species. Three were
small and two large, the *Giraffa jumae* and *Giraffa camelopardalis*; the latter is the giraffe we all know today. Fossils of *Giraffa
camelopardalis*, the modern giraffe with its long neck, appear in
East Africa from one million years ago onwards. Why all these
different species (over thirty) all disappeared we can only conjec-
ture, as many other ruminant species like the deer and antelope
grew and spread worldwide. It may be that a peculiar and as yet
unidentified pressure led to the modern giraffe having to
become the specialist browser of today in order to survive.

The okapi shares many giraffine features: long face, two frontal horns, big ears and sloped back. Living in the African equatorial rainforest, there is plenty of lush vegetation to eat so the okapi does not need a long neck.

The okapi, with its short neck and legs, is more representative of its ancestors and has survived virtually unchanged because of its geographical and ecological isolation in the equatorial forests of the Congo. It remained undiscovered by zoologists until Victorian times, when explorers from the 1880s onwards heard rumours of a peculiar striped donkey or 'Atti or O'api', which was finally recognized as a new species, the okapi (*Okapi jonstoni*) in 1901.[6]

The early Victorian exploration of the African heartland and savannahs focussed European attention on the giraffe in its natural habitat, and soon regional variations in coat patterns or pelage were reported. At first these variants were thought to represent different species but gradually the opinion formed that

A close-up of a giraffe's flank showing the almost geometrical pattern of its skin. Note the covering of short hair.

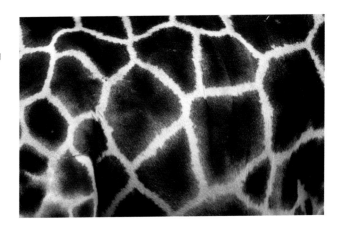

they represented different sub-species or races of the single species *Giraffa camelopardalis*. These sub-species (ranging from seven to fifteen) were named either after their location in Africa, like the Western giraffe (*Giraffa camelopardalis peralta*); after the zoologist who first described them, like Rothschild's giraffe (*Giraffa camelopardalis rothschildi*), named after Lord Rothschild, and Thornicroft's giraffe (*Giraffa camelopardalis thonicrofti*); or for their coat pattern (pelage), like the Reticulated giraffe (*Giraffa camelopardalis reticulate*). The two (presumed) sub-species with the most distinctive coat patterns are the Maasai giraffe, which has been described as 'jagged-edged, vine leaf shaped spots of dark chocolate on a yellowish background'[7] and the Reticulated giraffe, with its polygonal blocks of brown on white.

It was thought that the freedom of the early giraffe to roam across Africa was altered over time by changes in the climate and the creation of geographical barriers like lakes and forests, which isolated certain populations and led to the evolution of specific sub-species.

In the past few years genetic studies were started that attempted to pin down the taxonomy and phylogeography of the different giraffe sub-specics and to everyone's amazement it has now been found that there are in fact six (possibly seven) distinct species, the Angolan, Maasai, Reticulated, Rothschild's, South African and Western giraffes.[8] What had previously been considered sub-species, like the Maasai and Reticulated giraffes, are so genetically distinct that they deserve to be classified as species in their own right. This finding is surprising because when giraffes from these distinct regions are kept in captivity, they will interbreed. Furthermore, some of these giraffes are not geographically isolated and since they are able to cover large distances (hundreds of kilometres) across scrub and savannah, they should be able to interbreed in the wild. Both factors should ultimately lead towards a single species. The giraffe is a social

The current distribution of giraffe across Africa, showing the different coat patterns and a genetic map of the relationships between the different populations.

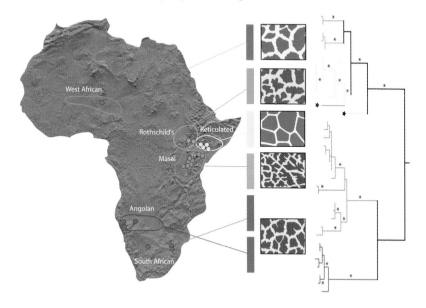

A tall bull giraffe, with its long neck allowing it to spot other giraffe and potential predators.

animal and is likely to stay in small herds; it may be this behaviour that has led to genetic isolation rather than geographical isolation in the wild. In captivity, the giraffe's social behaviour may also change so as to favour hybridization.

One of the authors of this genetic study, a Mr Brown, when interviewed, put it simply: 'The female Maasai giraffe may be looking at the male reticulated giraffe and thinking 'I don't like you: I don't want to mate with you'.' The total number of giraffes in the wild has been estimated to be around 100,000, which, considering the pressures of human encroachment, is sustainable. When viewing this population as six individual species, some of the six species may be considered endangered; the Western giraffe, which used to be called the Nigerian Giraffe, is actually extinct in Nigeria, and only around 200 individuals are thought to exist in Niger, while only a few hundred Rothschild's giraffes survive in protected areas of Kenya and Uganda.

Unfortunately, zoos, the traditional curators of endangered species, have not thought to breed pure-bred giraffes and until recently most exhibited hybrids. If some giraffe species are now on the endangered species list, let us hope that is not too late to save them from extinction.

How the giraffe got its long neck, its most distinctive feature, is still unknown. No clues can be found from the many fossil specimens and the complete lack of any intermediate forms with a medium-length neck has left the argument open to theory and speculation. The 'tall tale' of the evolution of the giraffe's neck begins with Jean-Baptiste Lamarck, who in 1809 stated:

> It is interesting to observe the result of habit in the peculiar shape and size of the giraffe: this animal, the tallest of the mammals, is known to live in the interior of Africa in places where the soil is nearly always arid and barren, so that it is obliged to browse on the leaves of trees and to make constant efforts to reach them. From this habit long maintained in all its race, it has resulted that the animal's forelegs have become longer than its hind-legs, and that its neck is lengthened to such a degree that the giraffe, without standing up on its hind-legs, attains a height of six metres.[9]

He postulated that organisms changed by adapting to their environment, rather than through divine intervention; that is to say that through functional adaptation the neck got longer and longer the more it was stretched. This theory lay unchallenged until a little over sixty years later, when Charles Darwin commented on giraffe evolution in the sixth edition of his seminal book *The Origin of Species*:

The giraffe, by its lofty stature, much elongated neck, fore-legs, head and tongue, has its whole frame beautifully adapted for browsing on the higher branches of trees. It can thus obtain food beyond the reach of other hoofed animals inhabiting the same country; and this must be a great advantage to it during dearths . . . So under nature with the nascent giraffe, the individuals which were the highest browsers and were able during dearth to reach even an inch or two above the others, will often have been preserved; for they will have roamed over the whole country in search of food . . . Those individuals which had some one part or several parts of their bodies rather more elongated than usual, would generally have survived. These will have intercrossed and left offspring, either inheriting the same bodily peculiarities, or with a tendency to vary again in the same manner; while the individuals less favoured in the same respects will have been the most liable to perish . . . By this process long-continued, which exactly corresponds with what I have called unconscious selection by man, combined, no doubt, in a most important manner with the inherited effects of the increased use of parts, it seems to me almost certain that an ordinary hoofed quadruped might be converted into a giraffe.[10]

Put simply, it is survival of the fittest: only those giraffes with the longest necks would be able to out-compete their fellow giraffes when food was in short supply. Over the next century this simple idea became accepted as dogma, and remained one of the cornerstones of evolutionary theory and behavioural biology. Darwin also pointed out that greater height would allow better protection from lions, as would greater bulk and longer

legs. These ideas were postulated before the okapi was discovered, but the okapi supports this theory; it does not need a long neck to survive, as it lives in the lush tropical rainforest where there is plenty of edible foliage at ground level, with little or no competition from large herbivores or predators.

Criticism of evolution through selective competition for food increased over the twentieth century. Why didn't other herbivores develop similar necks to the giraffe when under pressure? Observations of feeding giraffes show that they often feed from low shrubs and hold their necks horizontally for fifty per cent of the time.[11] Another theory, postulated in 1996, suggested that neck sparring, in which bull giraffes club each other with their horns and bony heads, provides a more straightforward mechanism for favouring neck elongation. Fighting for females in this way imposes a sexual selection pressure, as those with the longest and strongest necks will be more successful at breeding and produce more offspring. This is an attractive theory but has yet to be proved. Recent studies have shown that there may be no difference in the relative neck size of males and females. Males simply have larger necks because they are heavier, but between the sexes the rate of growth is the same. For neck size to provide a selection pressure, then the ratio between neck length and leg length would be greater in males, which is not the case.[12] In fact it could be a combination of all these theories.[13]

Other factors, such as having a long prehensile tongue and flexible lips, may provide a selection pressure for a longer neck. It seems more than likely that over aeons of time, myriads of small changes add up over thousands of generations to the animal we see today; a view supported by Darwin, who states in an adjoining paragraph to the one quoted above that 'The preservation of each species can rarely be determined by any one advantage, but by the union of all great and small.' A group from South Africa have reanalysed the size of the back and neck bones of the giraffe and related animals such as the okapi and camel, along with fossil giraffids, in order to shed more light on the matter.[14] They conclude that the neck could only elongate by the enlargement of all seven of its neck bones or cervical vertebrae, so the giraffe must have extra large bones, which account for over half the length of the backbone. This elongation is different to the elongation seen in other ungulates like the camel and llama and truly represents a longer neck, since proportionally the seven vertebrae make up over 50 per cent of the total backbone length; in camels, the neck vertebrae represent only 40 per cent of the total.

It seems that this elongation had largely already taken place by the first appearance of the genus Giraffa in Asia and Africa at the end of the Miocene. Soon after this, in the early Pliocene (seven million years ago), Giraffa of modern proportions were found in the eastern and sub-Saharan Africa. This allows a two-million-year period in which the giraffe neck elongated. Calculations show that if we allow for a five-year generation time (the time between birth and first birth of a calf), then in 400,000 generations the neck would only have to elongate by 0.7 micrometres (hundredths of a centimetre) per generation. If we apply this time frame to 'punctuated' or stepped evolution (in which changes take place at random times within a single generation), with a step occurring every ten millennia, covering around 2,000 generations, such a short period would be invisible in the fossil record. In this case the neck would only have to increase by 143 micrometres per step. What is more, these punctuated changes would be effected during embryonic development, allowing greater differentiation of the tissue towards development into the cervical vertebrae. Current knowledge on fossil giraffids on factors which currently influence the giraffe's embryological

A Reticulated giraffe from Kenya using its neck to feed on foliage not available to smaller animals.

development does not allow us to champion either the gradualistic (microevolution) or punctuated route to its long neck. Only future research will tell.

In the early Pliocene the evolution of the okapi diverged from the giraffe. It evolved along a different pathway, facing different pressures on its survival, while the camel and llama necks became elongated, probably for different reasons to the giraffe: an example of parallel evolution.

The major criticism still remains in that there is a dearth of fossils; but still, the giraffe's 'missing link' has not been found or may never be found, if microevolution took place. Confirming the nature of these intermediate forms is needed in order to explain how the giraffe suddenly became the tallest animal on earth. It may be the new science of epigenetics, which joins Lamarck's and Darwin's theories together, that provides the final clue to why the giraffe is so special.

2 The Giraffe Inside and Out

The herbivorous giraffe is perfectly adapted to living in a hot semi-arid environment and in its African domains survives alongside many other competing herbivores like antelope and zebra. To survive in this highly competitive environment it has evolved into its own special niche. The animal exhibits a raft of unique features that literally place it 'head and shoulders' above its fellow competitors. With its two-metre-long neck and its specially adapted head and mouth, it can browse on the highest and toughest of savannah vegetation with a diet of over one hundred different plants, seeds, fruits and pods. Its staple diet is the thorny acacia tree, whose succulent leaves provide the giraffe with most of its nutritional and fluid needs. Like most herbivores, it is a sociable animal and is often found browsing in matriarchal groups of around a dozen.

A bull giraffe can be up to five and half metres tall and weigh up to 1,300 kilograms, with cows being a metre shorter and lighter. Of this total height, the legs occupy around two metres, while the body occupies around one metre and the neck the rest. Accommodating this odd mixture of parts has required the giraffe to push the boundaries of mammalian architecture and structure to their limits. Being the tallest animal has particularly stretched the design of the cardiovascular system. In most mammals the vertical distance between the heart and head is

at most several centimetres, but in the giraffe the difference is huge at a couple of metres.

At rest the heart has to pump around 60 litres of blood around the body every minute. Several litres of this blood must go to the brain to maintain a cerebral blood pressure of around 100 millimetres of mercury (to maintain the atmospheric pressure, which is around 760 millimetres of mercury at sea level). This pressure drives the blood through the cranial circulation. The blood flow must be sufficient to maintain the supply of oxygen to the brain cells for the animal to remain conscious. However, to achieve this unexceptional cranial pressure the heart has to work at a much higher pressure of 180 to 247 millimetres of mercury, the highest in the animal kingdom, and a dangerously high pressure in humans.[1] The giraffe heart is big,

40 centimetres in length and weighing around ten kilograms in a large bull, and beats around 70 times per minute at rest. This is in keeping with the size of the animal. What is unusual about the heart is the thickness of its walls: the left ventricle wall can be six centimetres across, with the wall thickness increasing

Drinking at the waterhole. While the straight rear legs support the animal's bulk, the front legs are splayed sideways, allowing the giraffe to lower its head without leaning forward.

proportionally with the length of neck, and hence arterial blood pressure. The matter of maintaining the correct cerebral pressure becomes even more important when the giraffe lowers its head: for example, a bull has to lower its head by five metres when drinking at a watering hole.

Lowering its head could potentially cause a cerebral haemorrhage (or stroke) as the pressure could climb dangerously high. The giraffe overcomes this problem by the blood vessels in the brain contracting rapidly when the head is lowered, reducing blood flow and excess pressure in the brain. Valves in the neck veins prevent backflow, and around 2.5 litres of blood is pooled in the neck.[2]

The next potential problem occurs when raising the head back to the upright position, as the brain could become under-perfused and the animal could become dizzy and faint. Again the giraffe circulation is specially adapted, and blood is kept in the brain and prevented from rushing straight back into the heart by special bands of contractible muscle surrounding sections of its neck veins. These bands control flow by altering the diameter of the veins just before the blood enters the heart. The thick skin around the neck also helps to maintain pressure by preventing the neck tissue from bulging.

The exact mechanisms by which the giraffe manages its blood pressure so precisely is still an area of active research; it is hoped that if we can discover how the giraffe survives such high pressure then we may be able to glean some benefits for humans with hypertension. The feet, two metres below the heart, which support over one tonne of animal, experience even higher blood pressures. Thus to prevent oedema (fluid accumulation) the small arteries in the legs have to have extra thick walls which are up to six times thicker than the arterial vessels in the head. As a consequence their internal diameter is reduced and can be six

A close-up of the eye shows its position at the rear of the head, providing good all-round vision. Note the bushy eyebrow in front of the eye.

times narrower.[3] A further adaption is provided by the legs being wrapped in tight skin, which acts like a pressure stocking.[4] What happens to the blood pressure and cardiovascular system when a giraffe is galloping at speed can only be guessed at, as cardiac output can easily triple during exercise. There are still plenty of surprises waiting to be discovered in connection with the giraffe's cardiovascular system.

Whenever you see a giraffe, take a close look up at its large lustrous eyes and long eyelashes. Its eyes, mounted on either side of the head, bulge outwards, giving the giraffe the peripheral vision it needs to look out for predators. If you look at a giraffe from behind you can still see the shiny surface of its eyeball. It has the largest diameter eyeball of any African mammal at 51 millimetres, allowing it to spot danger from up to two kilometres away. Apart from the obvious advantages of having eyes five metres above ground level, there are also disadvantages when running and walking. While walking the giraffe has to

The giraffe's prehensile tongue allows it to strip the leaves off tough, even thorny plants.

look down at its feet and a few metres ahead simultaneously. To enable the giraffe to do this the eye has developed its own special arrangement of light sensing cells, a unique arrangement that allows the animal to see ahead and the immediate foreground around its front feet, at a steep angle in front. This arrangement also provides good close-up vision, which helps with finding the most succulent shoots and leaves when feeding.[5] Giraffe have colour vision like ourselves, which is thought to be very useful when distinguishing if fruits and pods are ripe or not. A few observers have seen giraffe produce tears; whether this 'crying' is emotional or in response to irritants is not known.

Giraffes spend most of their time either actively browsing vegetation or chewing, so their mouths have to be particularly robust. The giraffe has an elongated jaw, with a grooved upper palate which has no front upper teeth. Of the 32 teeth on the lower jaw the canine teeth are lobed and splayed outwards, allowing them to grip branches. The molars are low and crowned and their surface is wrinkled and ridged, providing a rough surface for grinding (most mammals have smooth enamel covering their teeth).

Inside the mouth is another unique giraffine feature: its long, muscular and elastic black-purplish tongue. Being very long at 50 centimetres (second only to the ant-eater), and prehensile, it is used to grip branches and strip leaves, very much like an elephant's trunk. The tongue is also grooved with large papillae and bristles, which make it good for grooming and for licking up minerals and salt from mud licks. The dark pigment of the tongue is thought to protect it from the bright sunshine, and is sometimes absent in zoo-bred animals.[6] A thick, viscous sputum covers the tongue, which aids digestion. When a giraffe feeds excess salivation is common, and can be seen dribbling from their mouths.

The lips are thick-skinned and bristly, with the upper lip being the most flexible; being prehensile, it is able to grasp foliage. The lips are tough and seem to be immune to the sharp acacia thorns and the stinging ants that co-habit these trees. Where giraffes are common the trees soon become trimmed to giraffe height, giving a manicured appearance to the savannah.

The giraffe nostril has a muscular opening, allowing the animal to close its nose if it so wishes, helpful protection against sandstorms and the swarming ants found on acacia trees. The long tongue can be used to clean its nose.

On its crown, between its large ears, there are at least two horn-like structures called ossicones. These bony projections are covered by thick skin, with tufted black hairy tips, and in males can be twenty centimetres long and fifteen in circumference. Males have an extra ossicone (median horn), which is found in

A Reticulated bull giraffe with five ossicones. Apart from the two principal 'horns', one more can be seen on its bony forehead and two smaller secondary ones behind the ears.

the middle of the forehead just between the eyes; they are always smaller than the primary ossicones. Two more ossicones can grow on the skull just behind the ears in older males, making a total of five. The male uses its ossicones to club fellow bulls when fighting.

The ears are typical for a herbivore, being long (twenty centimetres), folded and pointed, with the ability to be moved independently. Giraffe have very sensitive hearing, moving their ears in the direction of the sound they find most interesting, like that of a predator for example, and often the whole herd will turn towards the noise once heard. Some observers believe that the giraffe is capable of hearing low-frequency sound, like elephants. This low-frequency sound travels many miles and allows communication across a few kilometres.

The giraffe is a quiet animal, for many years thought mute, with a repertory of sounds, described as moaning, rumbling, grunting, hissing and coughing noises, and making a snorting alarm when in danger. There is more vocalization between a calf and its mother: young calves will bleat and mew, while the cow will bellow when looking for her calf. Despite this, the most common noise you hear when you are in the presence of a giraffe is the swishing noise its tail makes as it swats flies.

The neck, one and half to two metres long, makes up one-third of the animal's height, and like all mammals' necks it consists of just seven vertebrae. These so-called cervical vertebrae have become enlarged at around 28 centimetres long (in man they are around five centimetres long). To enable the head to be lifted the first two vertebrae are articulated with ball and socket joints; in the giraffe this atlas–axis joint is modified, allowing the head to tilt vertically. This, along with its long tongue, allows the animal to reach branches an extra metre above its head. The fourth and fifth cervical vertebrae give anchorage to large muscles that support the head and neck. The neck muscles need to be quite large to support the head and weigh in at a massive 225 kilograms. Along the back of the neck is a neat, brown,

A close-up of the distinctive mane, consisting of short erect hairs.

stiff-haired mane. A giraffe's head can weigh seven kilograms in a large male and the skull contains the largest brain of any hoofed mammal, which despite its large size is similar in structure to its domesticated relative, the cow.[7]

The giraffe spends the majority of its day standing upright and foraging and only changes its posture when drinking, ruminating and sleeping. Though eating succulent acacia leaves provides the giraffe with most of its fluid intake, it does like to supplement this with water every now and then, and drinks about seven to eight litres a week. This supplement is not essential, however, as during droughts it can go without water for several weeks. Once at the waterside, drinking is a problem; the giraffe is a poor wader. It does not like entering the water and will only walk on solid ground. As its neck is not quite long enough to reach the water's surface it has to splay its front legs sideways. It does not kneel down, as it finds it difficult to stand up quickly from the kneeling position. To get itself up the giraffe has to swing its neck back and forth: first to raise itself on to its front knees, the next swing helps it raise itself onto its hind legs, and the final swing lets it straighten its front legs.

In the wild drinking is dangerous as it is then at its most vulnerable to predators, particularly crocodiles, which are capable of killing the giraffe by grabbing it by the throat when it bends down. Because of its avoidance of water, it does not bathe, and has to groom itself by licking and rubbing itself on rocks and trees. Unlike other animals, it cannot scratch itself with its hooves. A giraffe consequently carries ticks – five different types – particularly on its belly where the skin is at its thinnest. It relies on birds to remove these parasites and stands calmly as (red-billed) oxpecker birds climb over it doing their work. However, sometimes the birds will also pick at sores, so they are not always so welcome. Often oxpeckers are found sitting on a giraffe's back,

Red-billed oxpeckers are a welcome sight to any giraffe as they perform an essential service: removing blood-sucking parasites such as ticks. Giraffe cannot scratch themselves, and relieve irritations by rubbing themselves against hard objects. They rely on these birds to remove parasites from inaccessible areas.

A group of young Maasai giraffe, Mikumi National Park, Tanzania, resting in the shade under a tree grazed by the taller adults.

and will give an alarm if a predator approaches. Giraffes also carry the usual internal parasites such as flukes and tapeworms.

The giraffe does lie down to sleep, like cows and sheep. Lying down is not easy, because of its long legs, and requires a careful approach. First, it has to spread its hind legs while lowering the neck to a horizontal position. Then, after placing its front legs, it falls onto its knees. Now it can reposition its hind legs before collapsing them down too. The giraffe then relaxes on its pelvis and rocks back and forth to ensure its weight is distributed comfortably. Then it can lower itself completely and lean over. The giraffe can then return its neck to the vertical. It can remain in this position for hours, chewing the cud; often several giraffes sit together when ruminating. While in this position the giraffe will doze, leaving its eyes open and unfocussed with its neck still upright but relaxed. During these short naps of around thirty minutes the heart rate slows down to around fifty beats per minute. When shorter periods (one to ten minutes) of deep sleep occur the head is rested on its rump or hind leg, with the necks positioned just like a sleeping swan.[8] They do sleep standing up as well, having miniature naps; if you see a giraffe standing perfectly still then it is most likely having a snooze. Often it will be roused by a noise and will twitch as it suddenly wakes up.

Foliage is low in nutrients and, like most ruminants, giraffes have to spend most of their day eating or ruminating. They need to eat around 30 kilograms daily. Cows spend 55 per cent of their time eating and are more selective than bulls, who graze for only 43 per cent of the time. The majority of the remaining time is largely spent ruminating. Cows will eat during twilight if the moon is bright enough. Apart from ruminating, bulls like to spend time looking for fertile females to mate with.

The stripped foliage is chewed only briefly before being swallowed and passed into the rumen the first of its four stomachs. After softening a bolus is regurgitated back into the mouth as cud, where it is chewed again. The cud is re-swallowed and the bolus transverses the second, third and fourth (abomasums) stomachs before passing through a relatively short small intestine followed by an extra long large intestine.[9] This lengthy passage allows all the moisture to be extracted, producing dry faeces.

One of my first close encounters with giraffes as a child was with a group of sitting ruminating giraffes chewing the cud. The jaw would move side to side, chewing for several minutes before making a big swallow, and the bolus of food could be seen travelling speedily down the neck. This would then be followed a few seconds later with a new bolus travelling back up in the opposite direction up the neck into the giraffe's mouth, which would then nonchalantly resume chewing. The same muscles that allow the cud to travel the few metres up and down the neck also propel the water up into the rumen when drinking.

Males, being tallest, feed on the highest branches, often reaching upwards, whereas females feed on the lower branches, bending forwards. This ensures that there is less competition between sexes. Cows need to remain in good nutritional health in order to maintain good breeding condition.

Giraffes have a good sense of smell, as the early European hunters found when trying to creep up on giraffes, even when they were upwind. Giraffes themselves smell strongly, described as a strong scent that can be smelled 250 metres downwind.[10] Some people find the smell pleasant while others don't; a Victorian hunter described the smell as that of 'a hive of heather honey in September', while another stated that bulls emit 'a most disagreeable musky, nauseating odour'. Chemical analysis of hair and skin excretions has revealed eleven volatile odiferous compounds, some of which prevent bacteria and fungal growth. One compound, cresol, is a tick repellent. Their breath is sweet-smelling and some think the scent would make a good perfume.[11]

Giraffe skin is extremely thick and tough, which helps to protect it from thorns and parasites. When chased a giraffe will run helter-skelter through thorn bushes without regard to injury, its skin torn but not punctured. A thick skin has the disadvantage of reducing heat loss. Therefore the giraffe has special patches of skin that act as thermal windows to allow extra heat loss. The skin is heavily pigmented and the mottled pattern provides very good camouflage, especially when seen motionless from a distance.[12] No two giraffes have the same pattern and therefore this can be used to identify individual animals. Sometimes extremes are born, which can be all black (all spots), all tan (no spots) and all white (with brown spots); apparently only a few actual albinos (pure white) have been reported. The giraffe body temperature is around 38–9°C and rather than perspire they lose heat directly via the skin.[13] Their body temperature rises during the day, only to fall during the cool of the night. They rarely seek shade but do spend the hottest part of the day resting and ruminating.

The giraffe breathes at a remarkably slow rate for its size, at around nine times per minute, drawing about nine litres of air in each breath; this ensures it can draw enough air down its long neck to provide enough oxygen even when it runs.[14] A giraffe can run as fast as a horse (56 kilometres per hour or 30 miles per hour), as the Arabs and early European hunters found; when they tried to hunt giraffes, they could only outrun them after the invention of petrol-driven vehicles. The giraffe's legs are of equal length but because of the sloping back the back legs look shorter. The thoracic vertebrae have dorsal spines, which give the back its sloped appearance. This apparent difference in leg length has been stated in many of the ancient texts. The bones

A startled group of female giraffes run to safety. Madikwe, South Africa.

35

of the front legs of the giraffe are coupled with the rib cage and provide a stable platform from which the giraffe can hold its head high to feed.

When walking it has a shambling stiff-legged gait, and moves both its right legs together followed by the opposite left legs. The only other mammal to do this is the camel, as most mammals move the front leg and opposite rear leg together when walking or trotting. The giraffe has large feet of up to 30 centimetres in diameter, with two wedge-shaped hoofs (fifteen centimetres high in males and ten in females) with no scent glands. The hoofs become chipped with age, and allow individual giraffes to be identified by their footprints. When running the giraffe changes its gait and runs by bringing its back and front legs together, with the hind legs staying outside the front legs, much like a rabbit. The head moves backwards and forwards like a swinging pendulum, helping the giraffe keep its balance while at the same time increase its speed. Many people remark at the strangeness of this rocking motion, especially when a whole herd are moving. The early Arab hunters, while mounted on horseback, would chase the giraffe and bring it down by cutting its long hamstring. This method of giraffe hunting was soon abandoned when the rifle was introduced. Despite their unwieldy looking bodies giraffe can jump, and have been observed jumping two-metre-high cattle fences. The legs can be swung defensively, the front legs both sideways and forwards, and the back ones can easily decapitate a lion or man when kicked backwards.

A giraffe's tail is special. It is very long at around one metre, with a black tassel on the end. The thick tassel hairs can also be one metre long, and often nearly touch the ground. This long length makes the tail a very effective fly swatter, which can flick insects off over most of the animal's rump. When flicked, the tail makes a swishing noise, often the only noise to be heard around

a herd of giraffe. When in danger it can be flicked as a warning sign. When running fast the tail is curled and lifted on the giraffe's back to keep it out of the way. For centuries it has had commercial value because it makes such a perfect fly swat, and the long tail hairs can be woven into bracelets.

The long tail with its equally long black hairs serves as an excellent fly swat. When running the tail is curled up onto the animal's back.

In the wild giraffe live between fifteen and twenty years (in captivity the record is 37 years). A social animal, it lives in small loose herds of about one or two dozen, although when first seen by Europeans in the eighteenth and nineteenth centuries herds consisted of hundreds. A group of giraffe are really best described as 'a collection of individuals that are less than a kilometre apart and moving in same general direction', with individuals joining and leaving the group throughout the day, rather than as a herd. Within these groups, a single giraffe may be close to five or six

A mother grazing
while her calf
nuzzles her neck.
Note the square
shape of the chest
as the mother
giraffe bends
her neck.

other individuals, forming a small network of associates.[15] The overall group size depends on the supply of food, with larger groups associated with the greatest food availability. When no predators are present, they spread out around twenty metres apart and during a day can range over 150 square kilometres. These groups form out of convenience, rather than through social bonding; healthy adults in groups are rarely killed by predators. The groups consist mainly of breeding females, young animals and grandparents. These groups are in found in open woodland, with the older giraffes found on the group perimeter, one remaining vigilant for lions. The bulls are more solitary. Older, more dominant bulls tend to stay in the same area, picking up receptive females as they pass through. The younger bulls range further in their quest to find a receptive female. The bulls which feed on their own can feed in areas of denser vegetation, as they do not need to be so vigilant as the giraffes with calves.[16] They do not enter dense woodland, however, as leopards can jump on their backs and their height becomes a hindrance.

Cows reach sexual maturity at four years old and breed until they are twenty years old; bulls reach sexual maturity later, at four to five years old, but don't usually get the opportunity to breed until seven or eight years old. Cows are on heat (in oestrus) for around a day every two weeks. Giraffes normally sniff and lick other when they meet, but bulls look for oestrus females by sniffing and tasting the cow's urine. Licking the cow's tail and rump encourages her to urinate. The more dominant the male the more likely the female is to respond, thus enhancing the more dominant bull's chances of breeding. Often a younger oestrus female may approach a dominant and hence older male and encourage him by rubbing her neck on the male's flank. The bull giraffe curls his upper lip and tastes the urine, known as the

flehmen response. This grimacing exposes the vomeronasal organ, which detects the relevant pheromones. If in oestrus, the bull closely follows the cow, for hours or even days, and coaxes the female by tapping the cow's hind leg with his front leg; he may rest his head on her flank, or try to mount. Once ready for mating, the receptive cow will remain still. The process of mating is over quickly. Once over the males quickly leave and looks for another receptive cow. There is no prolonged courtship, as males do not care for their young, and show no interest in their welfare once born. Breeding occurs all year round, but in some parts of Africa it peaks in the rainy season, allowing more births to occur in the dry season. The female brings up the baby on her own. The period of gestation is around fifteen months (or 457 days). There is thus about 20–23 months between births and a giraffe can have around ten calves in her lifetime. Usually a single calf is born, but twins have been recorded.

Usually a cow gives birth alone and will return to a favoured birthing spot for each successive birth. She gives birth standing up. Born legs first, weighing around 100 kilograms and around two metres tall, with its horns in place, the calf usually enters the world with a two-metre drop to the ground. At birth, the mother licks and cleans the newborn, encouraging the calf to stand and feed; usually within twenty minutes the calf can stand on its feet and within an hour can suckle. The mother will protect her calf from predators such as lions, cheetahs and leopards by standing between the predator and calf. Using her back legs, she will kick any predator that attempts to get too close. This kick is powerful enough to kill, and is an effective deterrent. Unfortunately the calf sometimes gets killed by misplaced kicks, and nearly 60 per cent of calves die from predation in their first year.[17]

The lactating mother needs to continue feeding to maintain her nutritional status so newborn giraffes who cannot feed themselves

are hidden away behind small bushes and will spend a lot of time on their own, lying down. Calves nurse for six to nine months but will also forage at three weeks. The mother shuns help and keeps other giraffes away. Then, as the calves grow, after a few weeks they are left in small groups (nurseries), allowing the cow to forage more widely. Calves may lie low in these groups as well. Mothers only nurse their own young but they take it in turns

A newly born calf, with just tufts for its ossicones.

between feeding bouts to oversee the calf crèches. The mother and calf spend the night together. The strongest bonding in giraffes exists between the mother and calf and the mother will defend her calf vigorously. Females with young old enough to browse by themselves are often found in less densely wooded areas, where it is easier to keep an eye on predators, while males and calfless females are found in more thickly wooded areas where the best food is found, making them better nourished and fitter for breeding.

When growing up young males spend time play-fighting for one to two hours a day, playing necking games and sparring with each other. This prepares them for adult life, where each male has to fight for dominance amongst his fellow giraffe. Sparring allows young giraffes to develop their combative skills without injuring themselves, and is rarely seen in older, more senior, dominant bulls. These bulls, usually with their extra ossicones, spend more time pursuing cows. Displacement behaviour occurs as males compete for oestrus females. This involves the dominant male staring intently or walking towards the male he wishes to displace; another technique is to try to stand taller. The submissive male will bow his head and ears and will walk away without fighting. If this does not work then fighting will follow. Fighting involves swinging their heads like clubs at each other, a behaviour called necking; their heads and ossicones can provide a hefty blow. Fighting is a more reckless pursuit than sparring; with sparring each animal takes it in turn to take a swing at one another, whereas when fighting the giraffes strike one another simultaneously, and thus injury is far more likely. A fight starts as they face each other full-on or come alongside each other. They then begin to slowly rub each other's necks, intertwining them and delivering soft blows with the head. The ears are flicked aggressively. They may lean against each other

as well; this posturing helps them to assess each others' strength. These fights do not achieve anything, except that the dominant bull is the animal that remains the most erect during the fighting. At the end, the dominant bull may climb on the loser's back.

A group of giraffes.

Apart from mating behaviour there is little interaction between the sexes. Likewise in females there is little social interaction. Calves look towards their mothers for parental care up to the age of two. When they are left together they interact much like lambs: they sniff, nose lick and gambol. The calves that grow up together spend more time together and the more stable groups of giraffes consist of mature females and immature individuals who have grown up together. Giraffes seem to be able to identify each other by smell, hence the nosing and sniffing.

The docile giraffe is an amazingly robust animal well adapted to its surroundings. Its unique anatomical features, such as its long neck and tongue, allow it to exploit a food source unavailable to its fellow animals, while its long legs enable it to escape danger when threatened by predators. In some aspects of its biology and lifestyle the giraffe could be considered bizarre, with its long tail and strange gait, but overall the giraffe is one of nature's success stories.

3 The Ancient Giraffe from the Stone Age to Victoria

Throughout antiquity man has co-existed with the giraffe in its African homeland, exploiting giraffes as a source of food and raw material, revering them as religious symbols, keeping them captive as curiosities and pets, and trading them as offerings of goodwill in diplomacy. This early history of the giraffe is quite remarkable.

Africa abounds with petroglyphs and rock art of the giraffe, which can be found in all corners of the continent. Some of the earliest of these engravings were made by the Kiffian people, a Palaeolithic society living around 8000 BC in what was a then a green lakeside site but is now an arid desert in Niger. They disappeared when the climate changed (around 6000 BC) and the desert took over, leaving their rock art and skeletal remains undiscovered until recently. The most amazing of these engravings consists of two six-metre tall giraffes; not only are they the biggest known giraffe engravings, but they are thought to be the biggest petroglyphs in the world.

In the eastern Saharan desert, the savannah survived for many more millennia, allowing giraffes and other herbivores to survive into the pre-dynastic times of the ancient Egyptians (~3000 BC). A recent survey of the Nile valley and the eastern desert of Egypt has found around 324 giraffe images at 66 sites.[1] These images show the giraffe in their natural habitat,

The Dabous giraffes. A male and female pair carved into the sandstone. The male is around 5 metres tall. French archaeologist Jean Clottes photographed this Neolithic (6,000–9,000 year old) engraving at Dabous Rock, in the Tenere Desert, Niger.

confirming that there was a suitably wet climate for vegetation and trees to grow. The side-view images are primitive, ranging from mere outlines to images showing distinct skin patterns. It has been suggested that the orientation of these giraffe images, which often face left and to the north, is significant, and that the giraffe could have been seen as a heliophor, a bearer of the sun-god. We shall probably never know whether these images have religious significance. Artefacts from this time that depict giraffes have also been found, a fine example being an ivory comb.

When we enter the dynastic period of the ancient Egyptians images of the giraffe appear in many tomb paintings. These

Pottery fragment with depiction of giraffe, from pre-dynastic Egypt, 3500 BC.

Shouldered Meroitic jar decorated with painted representations of three giraffes, trees and human figure; Sudan, 1st century.

A 5,000-year-old ceremonial slate palette from Hieraconopolis showing a palm tree surrounded by two giraffes (from the Egyptian 1st dynasty, 3100–2890 BC). These valued utensils were used to finely grind minerals for use in make-up.

A young giraffe depicted with a monkey around its neck in the tomb of Rekhmire, a Theban governor from c. 1500 BC.

remarkably lifelike images show realistic colouring and patterning. They are obviously drawn from life, most likely from domesticated subjects, since the wild giraffe would have been extinct in the Upper Nile by then as the climate had dried and the eastern desert formed. Curiously, often in these images there is an ape climbing the giraffe's neck and the giraffe is usually tethered. The way it is tethered is unusual; it has ropes around its front legs, rather than a halter or rein around its neck. What this giraffine and simian combination symbolizes is unknown; the ape could be added simply to emphasize the tree-like neck of the giraffe, or indeed the monkey and giraffe could be pets just sharing each others' company. What it does show, however, is that after 2000 BC the giraffe was a domesticated animal, maintained as a curiosity.

In 1500 BC the Pharaoh Queen Hatshepsut sponsored an expedition to Punt on the Red Sea coast, where a number of exotic and highly valued plants (frankincense and myrrh) and animals including a male giraffe were transported up the Red Sea coast in specially built flat-bottomed ships before being transported across the eastern desert to Thebes and exhibited in one of the world's first zoos. This period is when the giraffe appears with its own hieroglyph, with the old Egyptian word for giraffe being 'sr' becoming 'mmy' in the later dynasties; it is thought to be derived from the Ethiopian name Zarat or Arabic name Zarafa.[2] Apart from as a curiosity, the Egyptians valued the giraffe tail as a fly swat and wore its pelt, presumably for ceremonial occasions. The Egyptians' ability to ship giraffes from East Africa later allowed them to export the giraffe from Alexandria to ports around the Mediterranean right up until the nineteenth century.

In the third century BC the giraffe or Zemer is recorded in the Hebraic bible in Deuteronomy (14: 4–8) and Leviticus (11: 2–8), where edible or kosher animals are listed;

These are the beasts that you may eat: the ox, the sheep, the goat, the gazelle, the deer, the antelope, the ibex, the chamois, the bison, and the giraffe. You may thus eat every animal that has a true hoof that is cloven into two parts, and which chews its cud.[3]

In the modern King James version, the bison and giraffe are omitted, but clearly they are ruminants with split hoofs, unlike the camel or pig, which are not therefore edible. The Greek version, written in Alexandria and known as the Seventy, provides the first and it seems only reference to the giraffe or 'Camelopardalis' in early Hellenistic literature.

Intriguingly, it seems that the okapi was also known outside Africa around this time. The Persian king Xerxes I (r. 486–465 BC) sponsored expeditions to explore the source of the Nile and central Africa beyond. The Apadana or audience hall at Persepolis built by Xerxes in 470 BC has a set of bas-reliefs showing scenes of delegates who were brought back from these expeditions to pay tribute to the great king. One relief shows a group of African pygmies, one of whom is leading an okapi by a bridle. It was only the modern discovery of the okapi in 1901 that allowed archaeologists to correctly identify the animal, which was reported before then as 'a curiously foreshortened giraffe'. This shows that the geographical range of the okapi was much wider than today, and extended outside present-day Congo.[4] Further evidence of its greater geographical range comes from the ancient Masai people of East Africa, who have a god named Em Ba; his image resembles that of a hornless giraffe, or okapi.[5]

Later the ancient Greeks and Romans knew the giraffe well. To them it was the Camelopardalis, and this strange name is thought to derive from the belief that this unique animal was an unnatural cross between a camel and leopard. This logic can be found in Aristotle, who stated in his *History of Animals* (350 BC) that in Africa

> it would appear that in that country animals of diverse species meet at the watering places because of the rainless climate and there pair together; and that such pairs will often breed if they be nearly of the same size and have periods of gestation of the same length.[6]

It was implied that it was the uncouth behaviour of these animals that led to their formation, a theory which suited European scholars for the next millennia and removed the responsibility from the Christian God, whose own creatures were created on the fifth and sixth days of creation.[7] This odd belief in the giraffe's origin is reiterated by the Sicilian Timaeus, who wrote in 260 BC:

The giraffe is the most wonderful, both for the beauty of its form, and the extraordinary manner of its production. For they say that the giraffe proceeds from a female Ethiopian camel, a wild cow (the Addax, an antelope) and a male Hyena; for in Ethiopia, the male hyena pairing with a female camel, she gives birth to a young one partaking of the natures of both parents: and if this happens to be a male, and to pair in turn with a wild cow the result of this second cross is the giraffe.[8]

In Strabo's *Geographica* (23 AD) an interesting but second-hand description of the giraffe appears when describing the fauna of Arabia (XVI. 4.16):

In this region, also, are found camelopards, though they are in no respect like leopards; for the dappled marking of their skin is more like that of a fawnskin, which latter is flecked with spots, and their hinder parts are so much lower than their front parts that they appear to be seated on their tail-parts, which have the height of an ox, although their forelegs are no shorter than those of camels; and their necks rise high and straight up, their heads reaching much higher up than those of camels. On account of this lack of symmetry the speed of the animal cannot, I think, be so great as stated by Artemidorus, who says that its speed is not to be surpassed. Furthermore, it is not a wild beast, but rather a domesticated animal, for it shows no signs of wildness.

While the Greeks were busy describing the world's flora and fauna the ancient Romans were collecting animals for another reason: to illustrate the exotic spoils of conquered lands, and for purposes of entertainment, usually bloodthirsty entertainment. Often moments of national triumph would be celebrated by grand public processions and games at Rome in the Circus Maximus or the Coliseum, in which animals of all sorts, including elephants, lions, bears, hyenas, bulls and crocodiles, were either pitted against each other or fought with gladiators and were slaughtered in their hundreds.

In 46 BC the first giraffe was imported into Rome by Julius Caesar, fortunately for it as a 'curiosity' rather than for its ability to fight with other animals or gladiators. Cassius Dio, a contemporary, states in his Roman history, *Romaika* (235 AD):

> I will give an account of the so-called camelopard, because it was then for the first time introduced into Rome by Caesar and exhibited to all. This animal is in general a camel, except that it has sets of legs not of equal length. That is, its hind legs are shorter. Beginning from the rump its back grows gradually higher, appearing as if it would ascend indefinitely, until the most of its body reaching its loftiest point is supported on the front legs, while the neck stretches up to an unusual height. It has skin spotted like a leopard, and for this reason bears the name common to both animals. Such is the appearance of this beast.

Giraffes continued to appear in the Roman Circus Maximus for the next three centuries. It was clearly well known by then as

Roman mosaic from 5th-century Syria. A Nubian is shown leading a giraffe with a well-proportioned body but foreshortened neck. The scene is thought to depict a public game or festival.

Oppian, writing in AD 213, gives an accurate description of the giraffe, even describing its hair-tufted horns, its brilliant eyes and halting gait. By AD 247 Emperor Gordianus III had a menagerie containing ten giraffes, which were exhibited when celebrating the millennium of Rome's foundation. How widespread the knowledge of the giraffe was can be seen in a third-century Roman mosaic excavated in 1996 at Lod in Israel. On the floor of what remains of the main hall, there is a huge sumptuous mosaic made of the finest tesserae. On its northern end is shown a range of flora and fauna, and amongst the fauna is a perfectly proportioned giraffe, accurate in colour and coat pattern.

The Emperor Commodus (AD 161–192) was famed for personally brutally slaughtering hundreds of wild exotic animals in the arena. On one occasion, after killing two elephants and several rhinoceros, he killed a giraffe, an animal he thought most strange. Emperor Commodus was the first person in recorded history to commit girafficide.

After this period, the power of the Western Roman Empire began to wane and the centre of power shifted to Constantinople in the East. With this shift went the ability to show and keep giraffes. Consequently, the giraffe was not seen in Europe for another thousand years, until Fredrick II of Sicily was given one by the Egyptians. Indeed, as European history passed into the Dark Ages, the giraffe became a beast of legend akin to the unicorn and phoenix. The images left by the Ancient Egyptians and Romans also disappeared into obscurity until rediscovered and uncovered by modern archaeologists.

Over the first millennium AD overseas trade burgeoned between Arabia and North and East Africa, where the giraffe still existed in the wild. Despite this trade, little is recorded of the giraffe, which only begins to be mentioned from AD 900. The belief that the giraffe was an unnatural beast still persisted. In 1022 Ibn al-Faqih, an Arab geographer from Persia, described it:

> The giraffe lives in Nubia. It is said that it takes its place between the panther and the camel mare, that the panther mates with the latter who produces the giraffe. The giraffe has the stature of the camel, the head of a stag, hoof like those of a cattle, and a tail like a bird. Its fore legs have two callosities, while those are lacking in its hind legs. Its skin is panther-like and presents a marvellous sight.

Another later writer (Zakariyā al-Qazwini, 1203–1283) states 'Among its natural qualities are affection and sociableness. As Allah knew that it would derive its sustenance from trees, He created its fore legs longer than its hind ones to enable it to graze on them easily.'[9]

As the centuries passed Arabian references to the giraffe in literature were still few and far between but turned to being descriptive rather than speculating about its origins. In the zoological section of the *Nuzhut-al-Qulûb*, a Persian compendium of science written by Hamdullâh Mustaufînî Qazwî in 1340, the entry for the giraffe reads;

> The giraffe is said to have a neck like that of the camel, and a skin like that of the leopard, and four extremities like those of the cow; its forelegs are longer than its hind legs, but in the books of the philosophers they say nothing as to the advantage of this.[10]

To these Arabs a giraffe appearing in a dream foretold bad news about finance or property or of a wife's infidelity.

In 1292 a giraffe born in Cairo was successfully reared on cow's milk. This was an important breakthrough as it would provide a means for young giraffes to be shipped abroad: cows could always accompany the giraffe, and milk was available everywhere. This is probably the first record of giraffes giving birth in captivity or even being bred in captivity, as only juvenile giraffes were caught in the wild.

Marco Polo (1254–1324), the well-travelled Venetian explorer, says that he saw giraffes while on his travels in Arabia and the East African coast. When visiting Zanzibar he reports seeing giraffes and provides a typical description of the time:

> Elephants are produced in this country in wonderful profusion. There are also lions that are black and quite different from ours . . . They have also many giraffes. This is a beautiful creature, and I must give you a description of it. Its body is short and somewhat sloped to the rear,

for its hind legs are short whilst the fore-legs and the neck are both very long, and thus its head stands about three paces from the ground. The head is small, and the animal is not at all mischievous. Its colour is all red and white in round spots, and it is really a beautiful object.[11]

Whether this is an eye-witness account is hard to tell, but it seems more likely to be a second-hand description picked up during his travels around Asia.

At this time Arabia was the centre of world trade, being on the crossroads of many international trade routes between Europe, Africa and the Far East. It is here that travellers would hear of the giraffe. The earliest Chinese record appears at this time in 1215, when Zhao Rugua, a customs inspector at the city of Quanazhou, described the animal as having a leopard's neck, cow's hoofs and a tall neck: clearly a second-hand view![12] However, things changed dramatically in the fifteenth century when, after many years of isolation, the Chinese began to open the sea routes to the western world in order to explore the world for themselves. They sent a large fleet of around 62 ships and 37,000 troops westward, commanded by the admiral and eunuch Zheng He. During one of these voyages the first giraffes were seen in Bengal. A giraffe had been given as a coronation gift from the coastal state of Melindi (now Kenya), to the new King Saifud-din. Melindi was a prosperous trading post between Arabia and India. The Melindi ambassadors were persuaded by the Chinese to obtain another giraffe for the Chinese Emperor. Zheng He took his giraffe back to Beijing in 1415. No details are given as to how the giraffe was transported or how long the journey took, but on its arrival the giraffe caused a sensation as it was thought to be the mythical beast known as a unicorn or K'i-lin. It was thought that the K'i-lin only appeared at auspicious times, and

The giraffe presented to the Emperor of China in 1414, painted by Shen Tu in 1415.

provided proof that only a virtuous Emperor reigned. This creature was on a par with the dragon and phoenix. One of the courtiers explained;

> This shows that your Majesty's virtue equals that of heaven; its merciful blessings have spread far and wide so that its harmonious vapours have emanated a K'i-lin, as an endless bliss to the state for myriad, myriad years.[13]

This symbolic link ensured that the giraffe became a popular animal in China, and when another giraffe was sent directly from Melindi in 1421 the Emperor greeted the animal personally with great pomp and circumstance. These giraffes appear in many extant portraits of the time, which were only uncovered recently in the nineteenth and twentieth centuries.[14] Within a decade foreign trade and travel had become restricted and the giraffe's story ends in China until the twentieth century, with the re-appearance of the modern zoo. To the Chinese the giraffe had served to legitimize the Chinese hierarchy to the masses; this was not the last time the giraffe would be used to symbolize a munificent state.

The giraffe continued to be used as a diplomatic pawn, being received as a gracious gift and expected as a token of esteem by the eastern Roman Emperors, now based in Constantinople. It was here that many visiting Europeans saw the giraffe first-hand. One such person was John of Biclaro (born AD 540), bishop of Girona, who gave an eye-witness account of a giraffe being given as a gift to Emperor Justin II from a Maccuritae delegation from what is now northern Sudan.[15] Moving on through history, obscure references to the giraffe are made in the thirteenth century by the monk Vincent of Beauvais in his book *Speculum Naturale* (Mirror of Nature) and by Albertus Magnus in his great book *De Animalibus*. In the eleventh century Emperor Constantine XI was given a giraffe by the Sultan of Egypt, a practice that continued even after the 1453 Turkish conquest of Constantinople. In 1566 a giraffe formed part of the procession for the circumcision feast of Mohammed II. The Turks valued exotic animals like the giraffe and Constantinople became famed for its zoos, or seraglios, as they were known then.

Apart from the Sicilian Emperor Frederick II, who in 1250 swapped a white bear for a giraffe with the sultan of Egypt, it was not until the fifteenth century, in Italy, that the giraffe briefly splashed boldly back into history. At this time the Muslim east was seen as exotic and its art and culture considered desir-able and fashionable. Therefore when in 1486 the Burji Mamluk Sultan of Egypt, al-Ashraf Qaitbay, offered a giraffe to Lorenzo de' Medici in Florence it was considered a very valuable gift and therefore a great political gesture. Such a gift would confirm the grandeur of the Medici family. The family already had its own seraglio, containing lions, bears, wolves and wild boar, so a giraffe would be welcome. The Florentines were trading with the Turks, unlike the Venetians who were at war with the Turks and Mamluks (Egyptians), and in addition had their country occupied by the Turks. By offering the giraffe as a diplomatic gesture the Egyptians hoped that the Florentines would intervene with the Turks on their behalf in order to broker peace. From the moment it arrived, the giraffe was an instant celebrity, and provided a great deal of entertainment for the local populace. Just like later arrivals in Europe, it was eulogized in poems and works of art.

Anonymous depiction of Lorenzo de Medici's giraffe from around 1490.

This 16th-century fresco adorns the ceiling of the Lorenzo de Medici room in the Palazzo Vecchio, Florence. It depicts his triumphs in life, surrounded by ambassadors; his son is shown kneeling at the centre with Lorenzo's famous giraffe just behind. In this painting the giraffe is accompanied by its keeper.

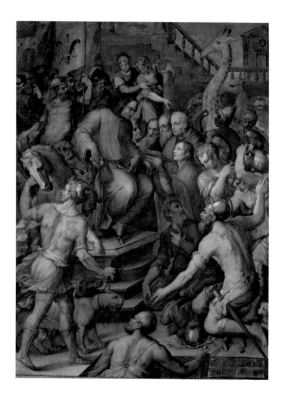

Amazingly, the giraffe was not confined to its enclosure but was allowed to roam on its own around Florence and was well known for its tameness. A contemporary of the time, Luca Landucci, wrote in his diary:

> I have seen it take sweetly from the hand of a very young little girls, bread grass, fruits and onions . . . I have also seen it raise its head up to those onlookers offering to it from their windows, because its head reaches as high as eleven feet, thus seeing it from afar the people think

that they are looking at a tower rather than animal. Ours appears to like the crowd, it is always peaceable and without fear, it even seems to watch with pleasure the people who come to look at it.[16]

The giraffe did not last long and broke its neck while in its specially built stable. This political gift did, however, feed the Florentine's thirst for the exotic and it was not many years before Florentine merchants such as Amerigo Vespucci left the Italian shores and began to explore the new world.

Images of the lone giraffe (most probably the Medici giraffe) appear in many paintings of this era. Most of these works have a religious theme, such as *The Adoration of the Magi* by Domenico Ghirlandaio (1485–90), part of a fresco cycle adorning the

This Renaissance painting from Florence is called *Vulcan and Aeolus* (1485–95) by Piero di Cosimo. The scene depicts man's discovery and utilization of fire (Vulcan, god of fire, at the anvil together with Aeolus, master of the winds, with the bellows).

Tornabuoni chapel in the church of Santa Maria Novella in Florence. In *The Gathering of Manna* by Francesco Bacchiacca (1540) a young giraffe's neck is seen to protrude from the melee of people and animals. Another work is *St Mark Preaching in Alexandria, Egypt* by Gentile Bellini (1504–7). Here a giraffe can be seen clearly in the background, and is based on sketches Bellini made while serving as a court painter to the sultan of Constantinople.[17]

A much more impressive giraffe can be found in *Vulcan and Aeolus* by Piero di Cosimo (1485–95). This work is thought to represent the dawn of civilization and the domestication of animals, represented by the horse, as a working animal, while the giraffe represents the domesticated pet or alternatively the

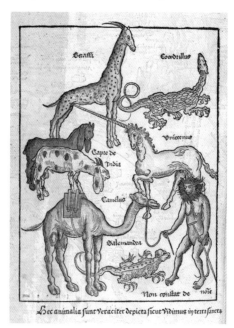

Erhard Reuwich, 'Opus Transmarine Peregrinationis' ('Travels to the Holy Land'), 1483, hand-coloured woodcut from Bernhard von Breydenbach's *Peregrinationes in Terram Sanctam* (1486). While the author may have seen these animals at the Sultan's menagerie in Cairo, the artist derived his image from an oral description.

An ink drawing of a giraffe in a 1470s manuscript of writings by Cyriacus D'Ancona, who travelled in Asia Minor in 1446. These images were copied by artists such as Bosch and Bellini.

wild animal. The famous work *The Garden of Earthly Delights*, a triptych painted by Hieronymus Bosch in 1503–4, depicts a white giraffe in the left panel which shows Adam and Eve in the Garden of Eden. This likeness is thought to have been copied from an illustration in an Egyptian travelogue of 1445 by Cyriacus d'Ancona.[18] The coat patterns and colours of these giraffes are close to life but the stance of the back legs always seems to be wrong, and often too low.

In the fifteenth century fine art was not to be seen by the general public but adorned the walls of rich benefactors. The printed monochrome image was the more common medium for educating the masses. The first woodcut images printed of the giraffe appearing at this time were unfortunately carved using

A woodcut by Niklas Stoer from 1529 depicting the Lorenzo de Medici giraffe. The inscription mistakenly attributes the gift as coming from a Turkish emperor, hence the attendant wearing Turkish clothes.

This giraffe drawn by Melchoir Luorgius at Constantinople in 1559 was the first image published in an English book, Edward Topsell's *Historie of Fourefooted Beastes* in 1607.

written descriptions rather than from life or art. These poor images were then copied by other woodcut artists and printers, which led to more and more bizarre images of the beast. A woodcut by Bernhard von Breydenbach, in his book *Peregrinationes in Terrum Sanctum*, printed in Mainz in 1486, shows the 'Seraffa' (derived from zarafa), which bears a slight resemblance to a giraffe but has the long pointed horns of an antelope, a horse's head and the rear end of a dog. A 1529 woodcut from Nuremburg does better and gives a good representation of the animal, which is bridled but is far too small at only six foot.

Between 1551 and 1587 the zoological encyclopaedia, *Historia Animaliu*, of Swiss Renaissance zoologist Conrad Gesner (1516–1565) was published, which contains an entry for the giraffe. To a modern viewer the image seems most odd, and it is clear that the artist had not personally observed a giraffe. When creating images from literal descriptions a lot can be lost in the translation process; clearly this has happened in this case. The coloured woodcut image looks more like a strange cross between

'Girafa', anonymous engraving of a tethered giraffe, first half of the 16th century.

A Flemish tapestry from Tournai of around 1500, *The Caravan of Giraffes*. The giraffes in these gypsy caravans have extra-long necks, and give no clue as to what contemporary giraffe images inspired the tapestry designer.

a dog and a goat, with its pointed horns and extended muscular neck, than a giraffe. A 1553 French woodcut by Pierre Belon (1517–1564) depicts a single male giraffe with a realistic head showing the ossicones and the cow-like ears. The lower body is less realistic, and is more like that of a camel. At the same time André Thevat's 1575 image is not giraffe-like: ossicones are shown but the body shape is all wrong because of the continuing misconception that the rear legs were shorter than the front legs.

These imagined images were common until the eighteenth century, when expeditions to the South African interior began. Explorers trekking inland from the Cape for the first time reported seeing these animals in groups and, more importantly, in their natural habitat. In 1663, in Namaqualand, a Dutch expedition party led by Jonas de la Guerre reported seeing two 'camels' which were most likely giraffes, for the old Dutch or Afrikaans word for giraffe was Kamel.[19] It was almost another hundred years before an expedition definitely reported seeing giraffes. In

1760 Jacobus Coetsé Jansz, who had travelled the furthest north, managed to shoot two females and returned to Cape Town with the pelt of a young animal. This stimulated further exploration, and in 1761 a state-sponsored expedition led by Captain Hendrik Hop and documented by Carel Frederik Brink headed north. It soon encountered a large female giraffe and its calf. After shooting the mother, the calf was reportedly kept alive for five days before dying. Eleven days later they successfully shot a bull giraffe, which was skinned. Its pelt was sent back to the University of Leiden, Holland. This was the first specimen to arrive in modern Europe and caused a lot of interest among the zoologists and academics of Europe.

With this specimen and others and with better field descriptions, more lifelike images of the giraffe begin to appear. Comte de Buffon (1707–1788), the French zoologist who sought to list all the world's known creatures, was the first to classify the giraffe as a species. The giraffe image in his magnum opus, the 44-volume *Natural History, General and Particular* of 1750, was drawn from eyewitness descriptions and from the skin of the Dutch specimen.

Comte de Buffon's giraffe of 1750.

'La Giraffe Mâle' from Carel Frederik Brink, *Nouvelle description du Cap de Bonne-Espérance* ...(1778).

John Webber (after an original drawing by Captain Gordon) *Kamela Leopards kill'd by Capn. Gordon at the Cape of Good Hope*, 1750–93, pencil and ink wash drawing.

The ossicones in this image are more bovine than giraffine. As the description was derived from an immature giraffe the ossicones would have been underdeveloped. Buffon made a guess as to what the adult giraffe ossicone would look like; this misconception was corrected in later editions of the book after adult giraffe skins had been returned to Europe (see p. 70).

An English draughtsman passing through the Cape between 1772 and 1775 copied a painting of a giraffe, which he improved using a giraffe skull. A few years later the Scotsman William Paterson led an expedition north to Caffraria and was successful in shooting a few giraffes. The animals were drawn and the skin, skull, some bones and the trachea of a male were presented to John Hunter, the famous surgeon and anatomist, in London. This was the first specimen to reach the United Kingdom. The French received their specimens following the expedition of François Le Valliant in 1783. He provided a collection of drawings and

A giraffe is approached by a hunter with a rifle, in this idealized etching by J. Tookey, after the English artist J. C. Ibbetson (1759–1817). The giraffe obligingly ignores the approach of the hunter. This image shows the sloped back and was most likely drawn from a museum specimen.

returned a pelt for the Muséum nationale d'Histoire naturelle in Paris. The skin was later stuffed and put on display.

In 1779 Robert Jacob Gordon, a Dutchman, undertook a series of expeditions into the interior of Cape Province along the lower course of the Orange river in Namaqualand. He meticulously recorded the number of giraffes he saw and their location. After shooting them, he planned to record each giraffe's dimensions and have sketches made, which would provide 'a perfect likeness'. Most of the giraffes he came across were lucky enough to avoid being shot but eventually two were killed a few weeks apart. The second giraffe's carcass, a male, was instantly eviscerated, and Gordon spent the night with the carcass to prevent wild animals from eating it. He complained that he was 'greatly inconvenienced by the ticks'. The next giraffe shot was skinned and its hide salted, ready for drying. He then returned to Cape Town with the hide and a complete skeleton. The drawings and

In this later edition of Buffon (1752) the image has been replaced with a more life-like one. The size, skin pattern and ossicones, now tufted with black hair, have been changed.

biological specimens were sent to the Professor of Natural History at Leiden University, J.N.S. Allamand, and to Aernout Vomaer, the Director of the Cabinet of Stadholder Willem V in The Hague. Vomaer was given some giraffe specimens because Gordon needed his permission to ship the samples to Holland. These specimens allowed Allamand to describe the structure of the whole giraffe for the first time. Colour plates produced at this time now showed realistic images of the giraffes.

Cheaper monochrome woodcut images continued to show the giraffe inaccurately. In the 1791 *General History of Quadrupeds* by Thomas Bewick (1753–1828) of Newcastle upon Tyne, the giraffe is shown roaming the English countryside and even has a slight hump on its back, perhaps in reference to its English name, camelopard. The French name of 'giraffe' took some time to be adopted across Europe and was not used universally until the twentieth century. Of course, native names continued to be used in Africa, where the Swahili name was and still is 'twiga'. The Bechuana name was 'tutla', in Matabele it was 'intulta'. The inhabitants of the North Kalahari called the giraffe Ñ'abē, pronounced ng'habe, which is similar to the Ethiopian name of Nabis reported by Pliny.[20]

Popular texts of the time continued to misrepresent the giraffe as no live specimens were reaching Europe. The idea that a horseman could ride under the giraffe seems an odd one but can be found in many texts of the era, for example from 1823:

As these creatures have been found eighteen feet high, and ten from the ground to the top of the shoulder, so, allowing three feet for depth of the body, seven feet remains, which is high enough to admit a man mounted on a medium-sized horse.[21]

It was scientific curiosity and a thirst for knowledge that gave the giraffe some worth. By the nineteenth century every serious collector wanted a specimen, and its skin and bones became highly prized. This inevitably led to the notion that live specimens would be even better. The next chapter describes how these first live giraffes appeared in Europe and in particular in England, France, Vienna and Turkey, and eventually came to virtually every country in the world.

4 The Giraffe Returns to Europe

At the dawn of the nineteenth century the only place to find living giraffes was in the wild, mostly far inland, away from the coastal regions and in the more arid, remoter, as yet unexplored parts of Africa. The Nile still provided the only known shipping route back to Europe for this tallest of creatures and over the next eighty years many Eastern giraffe were to be shipped via this route to populate the great zoos of Europe.

The early nineteenth century saw a scramble to colonize Africa. The establishment of ports and trading routes around the Cape of Good Hope in South Africa led to a large influx of explorers, both civilian and military, hoping to make their fortunes. Later in the century, with the building of steam railways, the interior of Africa became more accessible, allowing the sport of big game hunting to become easier and thus more popular. As railway and road access improved, along with the invention of the high-powered rifle, game hunting became ever easier and allowed those with the inclination and opportunity to shoot giraffes, slaughtering them in their thousands and driving the animal to the edge of extinction in just a few decades. Eventually professional hunters turned to being game suppliers and were able to make big profits catching and shipping live giraffes back to the European zoos.

The giraffe specimen given to Dr Hunter in 1780 was the first to reach England.[1] It had been shot in southeast Africa by

Giraffes from
*Portraits of the
Game and Wild
Animals of Southern
Africa Delineated
from Life in their
Native Haunts
by Captain W.
Cornwallis Harris*
(1840).

Lieutenant Paterson on a botanical expedition sponsored by Lady Strathmore, who presented Hunter with a specimen to add to his renowned collection.[2] A giraffe was a very welcome addition to his world-famous anatomy museum at Leicester Square. Dr Hunter said of the specimen:

> In point of its size, it is above eighteen feet high, with an erect neck and long feet, and in many respects partaking of the species of the camel. From stiffness of its joints, it can neither stoop, nor lie down; but as nature is ever provident for its creatures, it receives its food from the leaves of trees, which from its extreme height it can readily do by putting its head in among the branches.[3]

How Dr Hunter thought these 'stiff joints' would affect the giraffe's ability to drink water is not recorded.

A rare camelopard design hand-painted onto a soft paste porcelain milk jug, c. 1770.

Although a live specimen was still unknown in Europe, an English newspaper report from 1774 states that 'the camelopard, a very rare and scarce animal, is now on its passage as a present to Lord Clive'.[4] Clive of India was famed as the founder of British Indian empire, but in 1774 he committed suicide, so what happened to the giraffe, if it existed at all, is a mystery as it never reached the UK.

When the first live giraffe arrived in modern Europe is controversial. It has been stated that a giraffe was imported into London in 1805 by an animal dealer named George Wombwell, owner of a travelling menagerie; this would have been 'the first giraffe to walk upon English soil'. Wombwell had reportedly paid £1,000 for it and was hoping to show it around the country, where he would have been guaranteed to make a profit, but unfortunately the reports say he was in the process of having a special wagon made when it died only three weeks later.[5] There are no records of where the giraffe came from or how it was transported to London. Some modern commentators thought – wrongly, I believe – that this was the giraffe mentioned in George Eliot's 1866 novel, *Felix Holt, The Radical*:

> To Mr Pink the saddler, for example, until some distinct injury or benefit had accrued to him, the existence of the revising barrister was like the existence of the young giraffe which Wombwell had lately brought into those parts – it was to be contemplated and not criticised.

Looking back through the contemporary newspapers, there is some doubt as to the truth of Wombwell's claims, as later reports claim that it was not a giraffe but a white camel painted with yellow spots: a fraud that obviously worked well, as the public had never seen a real camelopard or giraffe before. The giraffe in George Eliot's novel is more likely one that he imported in the 1840s when it was easier to do so and many metropolitan zoos already had their own giraffe exhibits.

At this time, moving a live giraffe from Africa to Europe was not easy; not only would it be very expensive, but it would require the resources and collaboration of several governments, something then beyond the scope of the private purse. Thus it was probably not until 1826, when Mehmet Ali, Pasha of Egypt, decided to use the giraffe as a diplomatic gift, that the giraffe returned to Europe.

Mehmet Ali, needing to restore relations with France and Great Britain, had two giraffes to offer, one to the French king

La Giraffe est Presentée à
sa M. Charles X.

Charles x and the other to George iv of Britain. These promised
to be the first live giraffes to be seen in Europe for 350 years,
since the Medici giraffe. With this diplomacy in mind the Pasha
had in the autumn of 1824 already dispatched a team of Arab
hunters up the Nile, whose sole purpose was to capture young
giraffes. In December 1824 the two sibling giraffes were caught
and transported 3,000 kilometres down the Nile from Sennar
(now in Sudan) to Alexandria. Upon their arrival the Pasha
faced a dilemma, for the female was strong and in good health
while the male was more feeble. He had been injured on the
journey down the Nile, as for part of the journey he had been
lashed onto a camel's back for transport; he would bear the scars
for the rest of his life. Again, diplomacy came to the rescue and

the British and French Consuls drew lots for them. The French won and chose the healthy female, leaving the English with the unhealthy male.

The fallout after Napoleon's loss of power had left French –Egyptian relations tense. The national gifting of a giraffe was supposed to relieve the tension and show that Egypt wished no harm to France. The female giraffe was to be transported directly from Alexandria to Marseilles. After accepting the gift the French authorities approached the Muséum national d'Histoire naturelle, which in turn approached Étienne Geoffroy Saint-Hilaire, professor of mammalian zoology and supervisor of the royal zoo, putting him in charge of bringing the royal animal to Paris.[6]

On 29 September 1826 the French giraffe was shipped to Marseille via Crete and Sicily in a small ship named Les Deux Frères, along with several antelope and three Egyptian cows, which were to supply the 20–25 litres of milk the young giraffe needed each day. The brigantine arrived 25 days later on 23 October, but it was not until 31 October that it was quarantined on shore at the local prefecture's estate. The prefect, Comte Villeneuve-Bargemont, grew very fond of the giraffe, even taking it for afternoon walks in the area surrounding his estate. While looking after the king's gift the comte and comtesse entertained many dinner guests, who were shown the new addition, often to their great delight.

While overwintering in the South of France, the next phase of the journey was planned. The options considered were either to ship the giraffe up the Rhone, or take it by sea to Le Havre, from whence it could walk to Paris. Neither option seemed viable and both could endanger the giraffe's safety. Eventually it was decided that the safest option was to walk the animal nearly 900 kilometres to Paris. Geoffroy's main concern was that the public would need to be protected from the giraffe, but as it turned out the opposite was true. In May 1827, after Geoffroy had travelled to Marseilles, the journey began. The giraffe wore a blue waterproof coat decorated with the royal coat of arms, golden fleurs-de-lys.[7]

Its journey from Marseilles to Paris was followed with ever greater enthusiasm, with its fame growing the closer it got to its final destination. The entourage – the giraffe, the cows, the caged antelope and sheep, and Arab keepers – travelled slowly by road, following the Rhone north and covering around 22 kilometres per day. As news spread ahead of the travellers the crowds of spectators grew larger and local gendarmes had to be drafted in to protect the king's property.[8] Geoffroy would go on ahead to arrange accommodation for the group and make sure everything was safe. By 6 June they had reached Lyons, where they took a rest for four days. It is at this point that Geoffroy rather than the giraffe became ill, largely through stress and tiredness. After Lyons, they followed the River Saône north. At Chalons they left the river and travelled northwest over rising foothills towards Paris. Here the party became fatigued and much infighting occurred. By 24 June they were finally approaching the capital; advanced news of the giraffe's arrival was causing great excitement among the noble classes. The royal family would have liked to come and meet the giraffe but etiquette dictated that the giraffe had to come to the king and not the other way around. The last stop before Paris was Villeneuve-St-George; from here the crowds swelled for the final kilometres, many people travelling down the Seine by steamboat to get the first glimpse of the celebrated animal.

The next day she walked into Paris, led by her turbaned keepers, to her permanent home at the Jardin des Plantes. Her entry resembled the triumphal processions of ancient Rome. The animal was led by four attendants, followed by Professor Saint-Hilaire, her three cows and an antelope in a carriage, while the troops held back the pressing crowds. The giraffe was first housed in the orangery and then in the Rotunda, a building shaped like the cross of the Legion of Honour, created as a tribute to Napoleon. She was housed with other herbivores and looked after by her Arabian keepers, Atir and Hassan, who always wore traditional dress and even slept with the giraffe. At certain times

of the day she was taken for walks in the grounds, which proved a great attraction for the general public, with around 10,000 people a day flocking to see the spectacle. After six months around 600,000 visitors had visited the new celebrity. Such large visitor numbers required the careful marshalling of the public and visiting times for ticket-holders were eventually restricted to the afternoons only.

This fame was reflected in a huge production of memorabilia or 'giraffanalia', equivalent in scale to the commercial merchandizing of today's blockbuster films. The 'à la giraffe' craze led to countless drawings, articles, even poems and plays being created. The Parisian fashion spread widely:

A fresh portrait was published every week, representations of her, in various attitudes decorated every box, every fan and even the ribbons of ladies: and men and women wore gloves, shoes, waistcoats, gowns, bonnets of the same colour as the spots on her sides.[9]

Even in London, dresses made in 'camelopard yellow' and china depicting giraffes became all the rage.[10]

After three years the giraffe's popularity had waned, and by 1840 it had been joined by a second female giraffe. The royal giraffe eventually died in January 1845 and her carcass was sent

An 18th-century china plate decorated with three captive giraffes, posed in an unnatural tropical setting. One giraffe has an amulet around its neck.

An over-painted lithograph featuring a giraffe.

for dissection. It was mummified and exhibited at the museum La Rochelle, where its remains presumably lie to this day.

The second royal giraffe, the two-year-old male gifted to George IV, did not fare so well as his French sibling. After Alexandria, he was transported to Malta where he was quarantined. His host was the Governor Sir F. Ponsonby; the giraffe was kept at Ponsonby's villa, Sant' Antonio. The grounds were poorly vegetated, with only low shrubs and bushes, and provided little foliage for the giraffe to eat, so the two accompanying Arabian keepers fed the animal 'dry provender', a mixture of grain and milk from the accompanying Egyptian cows. The Mediterranean climate suited the giraffe, and it thrived there for six months until its newly built transport, the brig *Penelope*, arrived in May. The giraffe was placed in the hold with its head protruding out of the central hatch in the deck. Above deck it was surrounded by protective awnings of tarpaulins. The giraffe took all this

Jacques-Laurent Agasse, *The Nubian Giraffe*, 1827. Edward Cross, the curator of the zoo, is shown talking to the attendants, who are offering the giraffe a bowl of cow's milk (supplied by the original Egyptian cows, shown in the background). The harness or amulet is not shown in this informal portrait of George IV's giraffe while it was still healthy.

without any stress and arrived safely on the evening of 11 August 1827. It was unloaded by crane at the Duchy of Lancaster Wharf, near Waterloo Bridge, London.

The three-metre-tall giraffe was housed in a warehouse, where it rested after its long sea journey. This was not the ideal stable and he was visibly disturbed by the noisy crowd trying to glimpse him through the windows. On the Monday evening he was transported in a horse-drawn caravan, followed by its two Arab attendants, an interpreter, and two Egyptian cows, to the Royal menagerie at Windsor Park, where the King was eager to meet the new addition to his small collection. The animal, like all captive giraffes, was amiable and lively. He was fed 'ashleaves, oats,

William Heath, 'The State of the Giraffe', an 1829 hand-coloured caricature of the ailing royal giraffe set in Windsor Park, showing George IV and Lady Conyngham (the king's mistress) trying to lift the animal by pulley. Below it states 'little hope is now entertained of the recovery of the Giraffe – since the last attack he is unable to rise without assistance of the Slings'.

barley and beans' and prodigious amounts of milk (about fifteen to twenty litres a day). Over two years he grew fifty centimetres taller (about eighteen inches) and was a great exclusive pet of the King, Despite this loving care, the animal gradually sickened, eventually becoming so weak that it was unable to stand unaided. Thus in its sleeping quarters, slings were suspended from the ceiling, which were used to support the giraffe's abdomen so that during the day it could stand upright. A newspaper report of the time reported that the King was fonder of his giraffe than constitutional matters.

The King continues to manifest unusual solicitude relating to the health of the Giraffe. His Majesty visits the menagerie at Sandpit Gate nearly everyday and remains there a considerable length of time always with reference to the health of this rare animal which is considerably improved, in consequence of some suggestions relating to its food and treatment, made by the King himself; still it is doubted whether it will survive the end of the year.[11]

An 1827 cartoon of the royal giraffe when it first arrived in the UK plays on the name of 'camelopard', and shows George IV and Lady Conygham (riding side saddle) riding the giraffe as though it were a camel.

Soft paste porcelain models of giraffes, c. 1828, made to commemorate George IV's giraffe.

Despite the fact that the giraffe was not on public view, the public were still interested in its well-being. It was also viewed with great curiosity by members of the scientific community. This interest was fuelled by the press, who kept the public informed of the giraffe's progress. They also, however, used the declining health of the giraffe to parody the king's declining political popularity.

When the giraffe finally died in the autumn of 1829 King George was naturally upset, but such a rare animal was not to be wasted and the giraffe was dissected by the Chief Surgeon, Sir Everard Home. His dissection of its ruminant stomach formed the subject of the 1829 annual Croonian Lecture at the Royal Society. A wooden cast was also made and the skin mounted on it by the taxidermist John Gould.

A giraffe sent to Vienna by the Pasha a year later was kept at the palace of Schönbrunn, the summer home of Franz II, the Holy Roman Emperor. It caused a similar public sensation to the

French giraffe. Its arrival influenced fashion, the handicrafts industry and social life in Vienna and triggered record visitor numbers. In addition to influencing ladies' fashion the giraffe also inspired a hairstyle, and a perfume named 'A la Giraffe'. The craze did not stop there; a giraffe cake was invented, called 'Giraffeln', which remained popular with Viennese bakeries up until the beginning of the twentieth century. Even a 'giraffefest' was organized, with the giraffe's handler as guest of honour. The giraffe theme even extended to the theatre, inspiring Viennese theatre director and author Adolf Bäuerle to write the play *Die Giraffe in Wien oder alles à la Giraffe*, along with the composition of two musical pieces.[12]

The Turks were due to receive two animals from the Pasha but one died. The one remaining giraffe very nearly did not make it as the ship ran aground before reaching Constantinople. However it was landed safely and walked the remaining distance. There was chaos on the day of its arrival and no business was done as all the government officials and people of rank went along to see it.[13] It was kept in a menagerie off the Hippodrome, a large square, where it was exercised by its keeper and was not frightened by the large crowds which came to see it. After several weeks this lack of alarm encouraged the keeper to take it for walks further and further from its stables, even taking the beast down the narrowest side streets. The giraffe, which was around four metres tall, soon became accustomed to being fed at upper apartment windows, and would tap at the wooden lattice of some windows where it was used to being treated with titbits.[14] The giraffe was also paraded in front of foreign minsters and ambassadors; one eye-witness account by a Dr Walsh of one such occasion describes how all the '*corps diplomatique*' were introduced to the giraffe from a raised platform. Two grooms led the giraffe into a courtyard below. The account states how majestic the animal looked with its small head, astonishing length of neck and awkward gait. It was decorated with a 'splendid' body cloth, and its head decorated with amulets of blue beads. This was to protect it from the influence of the evil eye. The other Pasha giraffes also wore these blue amulets, which can be seen in some of the royal giraffe paintings. The narrative continues:

> But its most extraordinary attitude was when it attempted to eat. Some plates of rice and raisins were presented to it, of which it only tasted. It was more attracted by an acacia which happened to be growing in the area. It threw up and back its head; then taking the pinnate leaves in the curl of its tongue, it stripped the branches bare in a moment.[15]

Next, the giraffe was offered grass; this caused the giraffe to gradually splay its front legs until it was able to eat it. The observer thought this 'extravagant expansion of the legs' most unnatural and painful for the giraffe. The spectator then speculated that the giraffe, living in an arid climate, must never need to bend down for vegetation and must drink only by wading into deep water. This theory was supported by the fact that the keepers always raised its drinking vessel up high to accommodate the giraffe. The mildness of the creature and its affection for its attendants was commented upon: 'it came among us like a spaniel, put out its head to be caressed and seemed quite pleased with being stroked and patted.'[16]

The Pasha giraffes were all diplomatic gifts, given with no thought to the long-term health of the individual animals, something that would not be considered an issue at the time.

Giraffes were not be seen by the public in the UK until seven years later, in 1836, when a private organization, the Zoological Society of London, decided to import live giraffes. They would do this primarily out of scientific curiosity but also to make money through exhibiting them to the public. This marks the beginning of the modern era of the zoo-kept giraffe.

For many years, the society had been offering around £200 (then a significant sum) for any giraffe brought to London. It took a M. Thibaut, a Sudanese trader, two years to find, capture and transport these animals to London. In a letter to the Zoological Society, he describes in great detail his adventures of how the giraffes were captured and shipped to England [17]

After travelling from Cairo up the Nile the giraffe hunt started in 1834 in the Kordofan desert (now Western Sudan). Thibaut recruited the local Arabs to help him; they were all experienced at hunting giraffe for food and pelts. They soon found what they were looking for and on horseback chased two giraffes, a mother and calf, for three hours, with the giraffes eventually becoming fatigued. The mother could not be secured so she was 'put to the sword and killed for food'. Overnight the party feasted on giraffe, which Thibaut found 'to be excellent eating'. Next day the remaining giraffe (a youngster about nineteen months old) was tracked for several hours through dense scrub and trees, eventually being caught. This was quite a task, as the giraffe when chased can run headlong through the thorniest of vegetation without any harm due to its extremely thick skin. Once harnessed, the animal became tame after a few days, and even sucked the fingers of its captors. The giraffe was fed on camel's milk, a diet familiar to the Arab hunters. Once tame it followed the group of its own free will.

Four more were captured, but all died on the way back to civilization at Dongolah, leaving just the original calf. It took a further three months in the desert to capture three more young giraffes. The four giraffes, three males and one female, were then transported down the Nile to Cairo, then on to Alexandria. After 24 rough days at sea they arrived in Malta on 21 November. After spending 25 days in quarantine, they were shipped on to London, finally arriving in Blackwall on 23 May.

Two days later, at 3 am, their short walk to Regent's Park began. Each giraffe wore a halter and lead and was led by the Arab keepers, wearing their native clothes. The police, several members of the Zoological Society and Thibaut followed behind. To those lucky enough to see the cavalcade it was certainly a sight to remember. An eye-witness account describes the journey, stating that the animals slowly made their way to their new home, nibbling on the trees whenever they could. They were persuaded forward by being fed sugar, which they preferred to any foliage. The only incident occurred when the giraffe were spooked by a grazing cow; they refused to go past the animal until it was driven out of sight. The giraffes duly arrived at 6 am without any further incident.[18]

Procuring the four young giraffes was very expensive for the society: the total cost was £2,368. 3s. 1d, a considerable sum. However, these costs were soon recuperated many times over. Within the first two months of the animals going on display, entrance receipts often reached £120 a day, with total weekly takings remaining at £600 for some months afterwards.[19]

At the same time a rival zoo, the Surrey Zoological Gardens at Walworth on the south bank of the Thames, had tried to get three giraffes to London first, and had hired a faster steamboat at great expense to get them from Alexandria to London in only sixty days (with a short stop-over on Malta). Although Surrey

A hand-coloured lithograph of a Victorian zoo scene with a realistic portrayal of a giraffe with her calf. In the background a bear is being goaded by gentlemen visitors.

spent more than Regent's Park, they did not quite manage to win the race. However, this brought a further three animals into London, so by 1836 London had a population of seven East African giraffes; an impressive state of affairs that unfortunately did not last long.

The three giraffes at the Surrey Zoo soon died due to inadequate accommodation. Their housing was gas-lit, and with poor

An 1885 poster advertising the visit of a 'magnificent living giraffe's first visit to Liverpool'. Note the old fashioned name *Camelopardalis*, and despite being only thirteen feet tall, the giraffe is shown towering over its 'Nubian attendant'. The giraffe comes from the Surrey Zoological Gardens.

ventilation the noxious fumes inevitably proved fatal. It seems obvious to us today that such fumes would be harmful to wild animals and that it would be wise to protect such a valuable investment. Wombwell also purchased some giraffes around this time, which seem to have survived the 'confinement and fetid atmosphere of a travelling menagerie'.[20] Tragedy also struck the Regent's Park animals: despite excellent and clean accommodation, one of the males died soon after arrival. While raising its head it received a fatal blow to his head on some brickwork.

The remaining three thrived, and by June 1839 the female Zaida gave birth to a calf. Unfortunately it only lived for nine days, but it was the first giraffe to be born anywhere in the world outside Africa. In 1841 a second was born; this time it survived, and was shipped to the Dublin Zoological Gardens in 1844. This first ever transfer of a captive-bred giraffe between zoos was effected first by canal barge down the Thames and along the Kennet and Avon canal, and then via the Bristol Channel and across the Irish sea by boat. How the giraffe fared on this journey, especially while on the canal boat, has not been reported.

The two remaining males, Guiballah and Selim, died in 1846 and 1849 respectively. By this time Zaida had given birth to a male called Abbas Pasha, which in 1849 was sent to Antwerp Zoo. By 1851 the zoo contained five giraffes: Zaida, three of her offspring and a female imported from the wild.[21]

By 1856 the Surrey Zoological Gardens was finally closing down and its sole remaining giraffe (the zoo had replaced the group that died of asphyxiation) was sold to a European zoo for £250. At the dockside, when its was being lowered onto the ship's deck, the rig collapsed and the giraffe fell and died of a broken back. Its skin was sold for £25 instead.[22]

The fifty years after the arrival of the four Regent's Park giraffes was very successful. By 1867 seventeen calves had been born at the zoo, with seven more giraffes purchased by 1870. The UK was heralded as the leading giraffe centre in the zoological world (though a mere twenty years later all of the giraffes had died and the giraffe house at the zoo held only 'wild asses and ostriches'[23]). Then in 1895 'Daisy' was purchased and proved a great crowd-puller. On one visit made by the Prince and Princess of Wales, Daisy caused great mirth as she galloped around its enclosure, kicking and bucking. The press reported, 'It is a long time since the Prince enjoyed such a hearty fit of laughter as he did on that occasion.'[24]

In 1897 a male, a mate for Daisy, was given to Queen Victoria as a Diamond Jubilee present but sadly died as it was being released from its transport crate. Another male lasted only a few

A photograph of a young giraffe taken in 1854, one of the earliest known photographs of the giraffe.

weeks. Success finally came with the arrival of a third male, the first giraffe from South Africa.

An aged captive giraffe population now existed across Europe. Anderson Bryden, a sportsman turned explorer and wildlife expert, stated 'At the present there is absolutely not one to be had for love or money.'[25] The captive giraffe population wasn't particularly healthy as little was known about their biology; they received the same food as elephants, rhinos and antelopes, and were fed mainly on fresh hay, clover and grass. The German hunter Schilling, when seeing wild giraffe in Tanzania, remarked upon how 'so shapely and well-nourished' they looked in comparison to the captive European giraffe, which looked so emaciated in comparison, 'with their neck vertebrae protruding more and more'.[26]

The reason for this dearth of giraffes in European zoos was simply due to the unregulated hunting of giraffes. Throughout the nineteenth century many thousands of giraffe were slaughtered

94

for sport and their skins, which fetched about £3 to £4 each. As the twentieth century approached, the giraffe's extinction became a real possibility for the first time in history.

But as Africa becomes opened up year by year – almost month by month – these beautiful and defenceless animals must surely pass away. At the end of another century, our successors will probably, as they gaze at pictures of the extinct cameleopard, marvel that so extraordinary a creature could have lingered so late into the world's history. Yet another hundred years and their successors will be inclined to rank the giraffe among dragons, unicorns and other creatures of fable.[27]

This rarity drove the price of obtaining live giraffe ever higher, and in the 1890s organizing an expedition to capture a giraffe was estimated to cost around a thousand guineas per giraffe, a

A coloured lithograph of zoo animals and visiting Amerindians next to the carcass of a beached whale, the centrepiece of a travelling exhibition at Ostend, Belgium, 1857.

La Baleine d'Ostende
Visitée par l'Eléphant, la Giraffe les Osages et les Chinois.

cost too high for most zoos. The difficulty was not just capturing the animals but the logistics of returning them to Europe. Only young giraffes were captured, often still weaning, so a plentiful supply of milk was always required, which required a small herd of cows to be brought along. The giraffe were only found in arid land areas, so water would have to be carried both for the cows and the hunters. Then once the animal was captured, it would have to be transported a great distance to the nearest port.[28]

GIRAFFES IN THE WILD

By the early twentieth century big game hunting reached its zenith. In 1909 Theodore Roosevelt, the 26th president of the USA, along with his son Kermit and a large party of helpers, took an extensive hunting tour of the British Protectorates of East Africa. The tour's main purpose was to collect animal specimens for the museums of America. This gave him and his party sufficient excuse to shoot or 'collect' over a thousand animals, including nine giraffes. The encounters with giraffes are described in detail in his subsequent book about his travels, *African Game Trails* (1910). He describes how in one such encounter, after wounding a bull giraffe with a rifle shot at three hundred yards, he chases the animal on his horse until eventually catching up with his quarry and finally killing it with a single shot. In another more interesting encounter he was able to creep up to within three metres of a dozing female. As it was startled awake, it lashed out with its left foreleg, just missing Roosevelt by a whisker. As one modern giraffe conservationist stated, whether this miss was fortunate or unfortunate depends on your view of history.[29] The party then 'pelted her with sticks and clods of earth' until she cantered slowly away. Roosevelt thought it would have been unfair to shoot an animal at such close quarters.

The party kept the pelts and skeletons, but often ate the animals for supper. Apart from complaining about the number of ticks, Roosevelt reported that 'the giraffe's heart was good eating'. When not shooting animals with rifles they shot pictures instead, these pictures are some of the first of the giraffe living in its natural environment. The camera technology was primitive compared to today and the images could only be captured at a distance; the photographs show giraffe looking straight towards the lens but always on the horizon. These photographs reveal little detail and illustrate how difficult it is to sneak up on a herd of wild giraffe.

Another hunter, John McCutcheon, described the giraffe in his book *In Africa* (1910), as 'a creature of most amusing actions', and states that he saw extensive herds of around fifty animals. At this time it was illegal to kill game without a licence, which cost $50, but this did not stop McCutcheon, who considered that knowing a licencee was enough. Therefore when he serendipitously came across a large giraffe, he decided to try to direct it back to where the licencee was camped. Chasing the giraffe on horseback, he managed to keep the animal in view as it ran off in the direction of a bush fire. Thinking that the giraffe would stop at the wall of flames, he was confident that the quarry was his. On approaching the flames, the giraffe only hesitated slightly before jumping through them to safety. This did not put McCutcheon off and the horse and rider in close pursuit 'breasted the fire like a gazelle and after a brief blast of hot air and blinding smoke the chase was back on'. The chase continued for another two miles before the giraffe out-paced the horse and escaped to freedom. McCutcheon states: 'there was no deep regret at having lost him, for I felt particularly grateful to him for having given me the most exhilarating and most joyous ride I had in Africa.'[30]

Stereoscopic photograph of a zoo giraffe house, c. 1919.

As the first decade of the twentieth century passed, the tide of public opinion began to turn against giraffe hunting, illustrated by this encyclopaedia entry from 1911:

> The giraffe is ridden down and killed by a raking shot at the root of the tail; but except when required for food or specimens, the destruction of this inoffensive animal which offers no trophy of the chase, is to be deprecated. Great numbers are annually destroyed by professional skin hunters and their carcasses are left to rot.[31]

During the Second World War the wild giraffe population was left largely to itself and even managed to grow a little as big game hunters were needed elsewhere. It was a different story for the captive giraffe. Dozens of giraffes were killed during the war; Berlin Zoo lost two during a bombing raid in January, along with many other animals.[32] Elsewhere in another zoo a different fate awaited the giraffe. As food became scarce, there

98

was not enough to feed the animals, so those that could be eaten, like the giraffe, were slaughtered and butchered for meat.

After the Second World War East Africa was a different place. Kenyan farmers had taken over much of the fertile land, which was just beginning to be cultivated. To many farmers, the giraffe or twiga (the local Swahili name) was considered vermin since it damaged their crops and sometimes knocked down fences. Although it was illegal to shoot giraffes, and any carcasses belonged to the Crown (the British Government), this did not stop farmers shooting them and selling the meat on the black market. Further pressure on the population came from poachers, who killed giraffes for meat and more alarmingly for tourist souvenirs; giraffes were killed just for their tails, to sell whole as fly swats, or to make bracelets from the long black tail-hairs, while baby giraffes were killed for their skins and made into hearth rugs. The smaller calf pelts were most popular as they fitted the average tourist's living-room floor best. It seems that the tourists did not care how these products were obtained.

The giraffe would have soon been extinct in this region if it were not for a few farmers who began to protect the animals by providing them with a sanctuary on their own farms. Two of these farmers were A. Douglas and a Colonel Swinton-Home.[33] The giraffes given sanctuary were still free to roam and were thus still in danger of being killed. To prevent them being shot, Douglas proposed that he would buy each giraffe on his farm from the Kenyan government for a token price of ten shillings – a simple enough solution – but the 'downside' of this proposal was that since he was technically the owner of these giraffes, he was now liable for any damage they might cause to other farmers' property. On the positive side, the so-called 'Douglas solution' saved the local giraffe population from extermination. At this time, the early 1960s, the Kenyan government began to

Giraffe feeding; when surrounded by lush vegetation, the mottled camouflage is not so effective.

realize the value of its wild animals and stepped in, along with extra funding from the World Wildlife Fund. Fenced reserves were set up and game scouts helped prevent poaching. Today most giraffes in East Africa owe their existence to these national parks and game reserves. The giraffe was saved just in time before it disappeared forever, and its story in the twenty-first century is more positive, as we shall see next.

5 The Modern Giraffe

Visit any large zoo and the giraffe enclosures are always one of its main attractions. In almost all zoos the giraffe is the largest animal on display, and as such is included in the zoo's advertising literature. The iconic long neck fits well into the design of pamphlets, guide books and websites. Exhibiting giraffes in itself advertises to the public the fact that the animal park is worth a visit as it contains 'African game'. The arrival of a new giraffe calf at any zoo increases ticket sales and is sure to gain local newspaper coverage. Simply because of the economic worth, the number of captive giraffes is increasing. Improved knowledge has created more successful captive breeding programmes, better nutrition and healthier living conditions for the giraffe. Thus today most people are likely to see a giraffe in healthy condition in well-proportioned enclosures. This is good news but in the wild the opposite is true, with the giraffe's range and population shrinking further year by year.

Of the world's estimated 100,000 or so wild giraffes, around three-quarters are found in Kenya and Tanzania, with the remainder spread widely over Africa with other large populations in Botswana, Zimbabwe and South Africa.[1] In Niger, around two hundred wild giraffes (*G.c. perallya*) still survive, without any predators and living with the local people. Luckily, this population is closely watched and is on the increase.[2] In other areas

A street sign advertising the way to Berlin Zoo, Germany.

the story is not so positive; a recent study in the Maasai Mara National Reserve in southwestern Kenya has shown a 95 per cent decline in giraffe numbers. This is not because of climate change, but is instead due to the pressures associated with increased human settlement around the reserve.[3]

Today the number of captive giraffes in the world's zoos is around 1,300. With few giraffes being added from the wild, it is important to have a coordinated breeding programme in order to preserve genetic diversity and prevent the ill effects of inbreeding. Thus giraffe-keepers around the world have formed the International Giraffe Working Group (IGWG) to collate data about giraffe numbers in the wild and in the world's zoos. The

IGWG has created regional giraffe studbooks listing the linage of all captive giraffes. In the North American giraffe studbook of 2008 there were 605 giraffes (250 males and 355 females) listed in 143 zoos, while in the European studbook (2009), there were 754 animals registered, with the oldest animal being 30 years old. In Europe the Rothschild or Baringo (*G.c. rothschildi*) is the most common giraffe (41 per cent), with a total of 308 (122 males and 186 females) in 72 locations. The least common giraffes are the Maasai (*G.c. tippelskirchi*), with five animals (1 per cent) and the Angolan (*G.c. angolensis*), with twenty animals (3 per cent).[4] Before studbooks were established giraffe species were often allowed to interbreed. This uncoordinated breeding was for two reasons: firstly, it was easier to exchange excess animals between zoos that had space, and secondly as it was thought that the giraffe was a single species, hybridization was not an issue. Now breeding policy has changed and most hybrid giraffe are kept in single sex groups, with a view to eventually making the captive population pure-bred animals.

In some regions this is a problem, for example in Australia and New Zealand, which have about 81 animals on the stud book (2009) and a large hybrid population. The first Australian giraffe, a male, arrived in 1926 at Taronga Zoo, Sydney, imported directly from Africa, with further stock arriving later, but with no recent imports the number of hybrids has risen to near 70 per cent (56 animals) with only 25 being Rothschilds.

In the past 150 years the giraffe has arrived in zoos all over the world. In 1868 Budapest zoo received its first giraffe, while the first Russian giraffe arrived in St Petersburg by 1897. Germany received many giraffes around this time, supplied by Carl Hagenbeck, a live animal dealer, zookeeper and circus owner who in 1874 imported a record 35 giraffes into Hamburg. In India the British were instrumental in bringing the 'zoological

This 1972 view of the giraffes at London Zoo shows the animals being fed at ground level. Nowadays feed is placed at giraffe-head height. In the modern giraffe barn, the straw on the floor has been replaced by non-slip, easily washable hard surfaces.

garden' to the continent. The Indian Empire was administered from Calcutta, and was the official home of the British Governor General. One such official was Marquess Richard Wellesley (brother of the Duke of Wellington), who founded a menagerie at Barrackpore in the suburbs of Calcutta in 1800. Maintained by successive Governor Generals, it became the Zoological Gardens of Calcutta (now Alipore Zoo), which by the 1840s had giraffes.

The only continent with a low number of captive giraffes is Africa. In Egypt, which has the longest association with the giraffe, stretching back many millennia, the Giza zoo has kept giraffes since at least 1874, when it had seven,[5] whereas in South Africa the first zoo-born giraffe was born only in 2009 in Johannesburg Zoo.

In general, around the world, the news is good for the captive population; the number of all giraffe species is increasing, while the number of hybrids is purposely on the decline.

To breed captive giraffes you have to provide the appropriate environment and use good husbandry. Shelter and plenty of space are the first things a giraffe requires, particularly in the colder climates of the north. Leningrad Zoo in St Petersburg had a successful breeding programme in the 1950s and today the Kristiansand Zoo in Norway keeps giraffes. In both places the outside temperature certainly drops below freezing in winter. This must be the most northerly latitude for the captive giraffe and heated shelters are required for inclement weather.

The giraffe barn must be purposely built for these lofty creatures and must provide over six metres of headroom, with doors of a similar height. In many of the older metropolitan zoos you often find a giraffe house (often with an architectural award). When the royal giraffes were brought to Europe in the late 1820s,

A modern giraffe enclosure at Chester Zoo, UK. The giraffes have a grassy paddock to roam around surrounded with a moat. These giraffes seem content observing the visitors.

A young giraffe peeks out from the London zoo giraffe house. Giraffe need to be kept in heated accommodation in cold weather.

their new quarters were adapted from buildings already in use and were modified to accommodate their height and relatively delicate necks. These buildings were often basic cowsheds and stables and proved a danger to their occupants. The Regent's Park giraffes were the first to live in a purpose-built giraffe house. The architect Decimus Burton, who designed many London landmarks, was commissioned in 1827 to lay out the grounds and house the animals of the Regent's Park Zoo, which had only been founded the year before. The giraffe house was built in 1836–7 and is still in use today. Inside the building there is six and half metres of headroom and five-metre doors. It was extended in 1849–50 when wings were added, suffered bomb damage in the Second World War and underwent modernization in the early 1960s. This building is now listed as a UK national monument.

Another giraffe house given the same status is the one at Bristol Zoo (which no longer houses giraffe but okapi and gorillas instead). This Victorian mock gothic Tudor building is disguised as a house, with a gabled roof and first- and second-floor mock windows. Only around one side can the obligatory high doors be seen.

A new arrival in Sydney for Taronga Zoo, Australia after a four-day sea journey from Auckland Zoo, New Zealand. Here Ntombi (African for 'little girl') was 16 months old, 3 metres tall and weighed 500 kg.

Most modern zoos now have giraffe barns; though not interesting from an architectural view, they have great utility and are easier to clean and safer for the animals, allowing separation of animals for sleeping, quarantine and sickness and separate pens for pregnant and nursing females, calves and bulls. Increasingly they have raised indoor viewing galleries for the public. These indoor viewing areas are particularly good for cold climates. Giraffes with their large surface area are good at losing heat on the savannah, but at retaining heat when there is a cold wind. Walking on an icy surface is lethal for an animal with such long legs. The enclosure must be of sufficient size to allow the giraffe to walk around, and must be enclosed by a high fence, strong enough to support the weight of a leaning giraffe. Usually a simple moat is enough to prevent the giraffe from reaching the public. This separation is necessary, as experience has shown the giraffe to be an opportunistic feeder, and Victorian women with floral hats were often surprised to lose their headwear as they passed the giraffe enclosure.

The giraffe paddock is becoming even bigger in many zoos as zebras, antelopes and flightless birds are all kept together with giraffes (a recreation of the open savannah, though without predators and scavengers); a good example can be seen in San Francisco zoo. This development is to be commended as the giraffes seem happier, and it makes the exhibit more interesting for the visitor. To these paddocks, the raised walkway is now being added. These raised platforms are popular as they serve two purposes: they provide a better view of the animals and provide the opportunity, for a price, to hand-feed the giraffe with 'giraffe biscuits' or lettuce leaves. This raises the profile of the giraffe in the public's eye while raising much-needed income for the zoo.

In the mid-nineteenth century travelling menageries, human freak shows and bands of acrobats, clowns and trick horse riders began to work together. This gradually evolved into the travelling circus. These circuses very quickly became like those in ancient Rome, evolving into great public spectacles. Gaining the sobriquet of 'The Greatest Show on Earth', the most successful circuses started to tour internationally, crossing continents first by road and then by rail, as the great steam railway networks opened up across Europe and North America. The giraffe was included in the show for its oddity, although it was sometimes used as a performing animal, like the elephant or sea lion, and was trained to be saddled and ridden like a horse. Mostly it was included purely as a show animal, giving an exotic aura to the circus. When the circus was at its most popular large mammals such as the giraffe could only be seen in the large metropolitan zoos, so many people away from these centres had yet to see a giraffe. The travelling circus provided the masses with their only opportunity.

Fortunately, the docility of the giraffe and its herbivorous diet made it easy to keep, making it the perfect show animal. Not perfect in every sense though, as it did sometimes cause problems, especially when being transported. In one documented case, reported in 1957 in *Tracks: The Chesapeake and Ohio Railway Magazine*, a giraffe that was three inches too tall to fit under a low bridge was holding the train up and with it the next show, fifty miles from the venue. Not knowing what to do, a freight clearance expert was contacted, who recommended a simple solution. He suggested that they should drop a carrot into the giraffe's cage; then, as it bent down to eat the vegetable, the train driver should quickly open up the throttle, passing under the bridge before the carrot was finished. Apparently, it worked![6]

It was through the 'crowd-pulling' capacity of the travelling animal menageries and later the circus that the first live giraffes were brought to North America. In 1835 the only giraffe in the USA was a stuffed one at the Boston Museum. One circus showman, Rufus Welch, changed this: he had enough capital to fund an expedition to Africa to capture his own animals. By 1835–6 they had captured eleven animals in the Kalahari. By now the capture technique had been perfected, although it was still fraught with danger. The horseman would separate a female and her young from the herd, and then ride alongside the calf and lasso it around its neck. Once this was done, it was important to dismount and wrestle the calf down to the ground before it injured itself. Of the eleven, seven died on the long journey back to Cape Town, where two more died, one of an abscess and one while being loaded into the transport ship, *Prudent*. Of the two remaining, one nearly died in transit but eventually after great expense and 51 days at sea, the two arrived in New York on 7 June 1838, costing $10,000 each.[7] They were instantly put to work and were displayed first in New York and then all over the eastern States. Rival circus entrepreneurs Titus Angevine & Co. soon repeated the feat, with another giraffe, this time from the Sudan, arriving in 1839. These three animals were a success wherever they went, but by 1842 only one remained, being advertised as 'the only one living on the American continent'. One of these animals died of the 'cold weather'. It was not for another three decades that the first zoo-kept giraffes were exhibited by the Zoological Society of Philadelphia in 1874, when five males and one female were purchased.[8] The American giraffe population grew slowly, reaching around 50 by 1958.[9] The giraffe did not arrive in Canada until the 1950s and today only a few dozen exist in a handful of zoos.[10]

Between 1873 and 1914 Carl Hagenbeck had imported around 150 giraffes into European zoos and circuses. After his death in

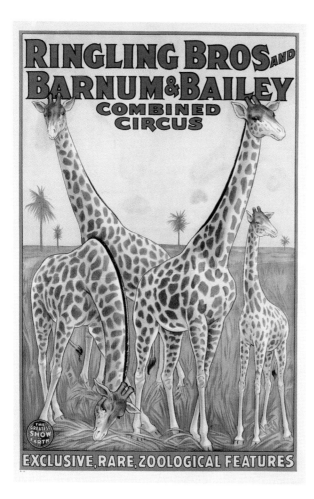

A Ringling Bros and Barnum and Bailey circus poster from 1928, curiously showing a giraffe eating grass.

1913 his son Lorenzo Hagenbeck continued the family business, on one notable occasion loading their circus with all its animals onto a ship and touring the world.[11] The circus arrived in Japan in 1933. The two female giraffes accompanying the circus were

A giraffe and horse circus act from 1982. The act was possibly inspired by the early descriptions of mounted rider being able to ride underneath a giraffe.

the first ever to be seen by the Japanese public and caused a great stir. Lorenzo describes how the 'the giraffe were invariably surrounded by classes of school children busily drawing, by photographers and astonished sight-seers'. The Japanese called the animals Kirin (derived from the ancient Chinese name). Before they left the Hagenbecks sold them to Ueno Park Zoo in Tokyo, where they continued to be very popular with visitors. Indeed, giraffes became very popular in Japan. Tama Zoo in Tokyo, which opened in 1958 and acquired two giraffes in 1962, became the second zoo in the world to breed one hundred giraffes by 1986, the first being Cheyenne Mountain Zoo in Colorado Springs, USA, which bred this number between 1960 and 1976.[12]

During the nineteenth and twentieth centuries all the famous circuses, like the Barnum Brothers in the USA, the Hagenbecks in Germany, and Chipperfield's and Billy Smart's in the UK, kept giraffes. Though it is not illegal to tour with wild animals in the UK the circus giraffe has largely disappeared here. This is not the case in Europe; a Dutch newspaper report from 2008 describes how in Rotterdam in the early hours of the morning, a rogue circus giraffe kicked open its pen and led a mass breakout of animals, including fifteen camels, two zebras and numerous llamas. The police soon rounded them all up and returned them to their pens with no harm done.

In 1966 in the UK the Chipperfields established a drive through Safari Park at Longleat, Wiltshire. Working together with the owner Lord Bath, the estate grounds soon became home to giraffes, lions, tigers, elephants and monkeys. Along with its historical Elizabethan house, Longleat was opened to the public, and was soon visited in large numbers. Other safari parks soon followed such as Woburn Abbey, Bedfordshire, owned by the Duke of Bedford (a previous Duke had kept giraffes at the grounds in 1899). The safari park provided a home for surplus circus animals and was innovative in that it was the public that

were now caged in their cars while the animals were free to roam in large paddocks. Safari parks have allowed giraffe to be kept in breeding groups. These artificial savannahs are popular all over the world, notably in Singapore and San Diego, USA. The small herds in these parks allow research into group dynamics and breeding preferences, which helps improve our knowledge about how giraffes socialize and live together.[13]

The keenest of 'giraffophiles' can even stay at the famous Giraffe Manor Hotel in Nairobi, Kenya. This popular tourist attraction is modelled on a Scottish hunting lodge. With its large windows and French doors, the giraffe can pop their heads in through the window or can be fed in the grounds. This hotel is the original house of Betty and Jock Leslie-Melville, who famously raised two giraffe, Daisy and Marlon, at the house in the 1970s.[14]

In Africa the national parks and game reserves now contain the majority of giraffes, and still remain the best way to see these magnificent animals. The giraffe thrives in the protected environment of the reserve, and provides the visitor the opportunity to see this noble beast in its natural surroundings, serving to remind us how strange and delicate the natural world can be.

A mother and her calf, Shani, in the giraffe house at Berlin Zoo.

6 The Cultural Giraffe

Today wherever we go we are surrounded by 'giraffernalia'; everywhere images of the giraffe can be found in all sizes, forms and colours. The modern giraffine image symbolizes many things: to some it symbolizes Africa, to others the fragility of species and the importance of biodiversity, to yet others it is a symbol of grounded vision, intuition, flexibility and far-sightedness. It is true that its exotic beauty, graceful shape, quiet and passive attitude, its elusive manner and long eyelashes give the giraffe a feminine quality.[1] Even the Victorian giraffe hunters hinted at its femininity; 'The most beautiful point about the giraffe is the eye, which is large, dark, full and of the most melting tenderness and shaded by long lashes.'[2]

This sentimentality fits with the ethos and code of hunting at the time. It was a masculine pursuit to tame and dominate Mother Nature, red in tooth and claw. Animals were seen as either domesticated or wild, violent or peaceful. There was no conflict in the Victorian mind between being a hunter and a conservationist. They were the same thing: the act of preservation and mounting of specimens, whether as museum exhibits or mounted trophy heads or skins, was considered conservation.[3]

After the ancient Egyptians and Romans it is only in Arab culture that the giraffe appears through the Dark Ages and up to the modern day. Arabian bestiaries, particularly from the thirteenth

An illustration from a Victorian natural history book expounding the view of Mother Nature as 'red in tooth and claw'.

century onwards, describe the giraffe's qualities and natural characteristics, signifying its strong cultural significance, with the giraffe's grace being compared to that of a beautiful woman.[4] Despite this, only a few images of Persian art that illustrate the giraffe have survived.[5] European artwork from these times also shows the giraffe, but these images are reconstructed from oral descriptions written by travellers returning from Arabia; a good example is found in *The Travels of Sir John Mandeville* (1371).[6]

The appearance of the giraffe in art, either naturalistic or abstract, really starts with the arrival of the Medici giraffe in the fifteenth century, as described in chapter Three. The Medici giraffe arrived in Italy just as the process of painting was going through a revolution. In medieval times pictures were painted on covered wooden panels or on wet plaster, the artist focusing on the principal subject, which were mostly of religious significance. Since pigment was expensive backgrounds were very simple and often monochromatic. The revolution came when more natural pigments became available, which allowed natural objects such as plants and animals to be included in compositions. Artists started painting in natural colours and using perspective, and while they still focused on religious themes (the main market for works of art) the backgrounds became filled with ever more exotic scenery, architecture, flora and fauna. This ensured that the Medici giraffe appeared in the artwork of numerous Italian schools.

In all of these Renaissance works a single giraffe is seen in the background. Often wearing a bridle and being led by an Arabian keeper, it is used, like the camel, to depict the Oriental exotic location of the Levant, where Jesus grew up. At this time, giraffes were seen more as biblical animals from the Middle East than as African, since historically they had been always been imported from Egypt. In Italy in the late fifteenth and sixteenth centuries the giraffe appeared in the background of several paintings, particularly in nativity scenes. Examples can be found in the *Adoration of the Magi* by the Italian painter Jacopo Ligozzi (1547–1627), and in the fresco *Adoration of the Magi* by Bernardino Luini (1525). A giraffe was included in the fresco painted by Giulio Romano (1492–1546) depicting the wedding feast between Cupid and Psyche. In the work *Christ in Glory with St Benedict, St Romauld, St Attinia, St Grecina and the*

Donor Abbot Buonvicini by Domenico Ghirlandaio (1492), a giraffe can be seen in the distance, being led to water. Whether these artists saw a live giraffe or copied it from other pictures is not easy to discern, as these images of giraffes are realistic enough easily to be recognized by those of us who are familiar with giraffes.

In later works depicting the Flood and Noah's Ark containing the world's flora and fauna, the giraffe is often included, but often on its own. The artists, not having seen both sexes, may have been reluctant to show a pair of giraffes in case there was an obvious difference between the male and female. Only in later images are they shown in pairs. Today the giraffe and the Ark go hand in hand. Virtually every modern representation of this biblical story – image, toys and models – includes a pair of giraffes. Artists depicting another biblical story, that of Adam and Eve and the Garden of Eden, had the opportunity to include a range of animals and sometimes included the giraffe, a trend that continues today. It seems that the giraffe has been adopted as a biblical animal, like the camel and donkey, not because it featured specifically in the Old Testament but more likely because of its brief appearance in Renaissance Italy.

In 1613 the giraffe gave its name to a constellation, Camelopardalis, and the name has remained to this day. At this time the far reaches of the world were still being explored and star maps were essential for navigation during long sea voyages. Employed by the Dutch East India Company, the Flemish clergyman turned astronomer and cartographer Petrus Plancius (1552–1622) received new star positions from the companies' voyagers on their return home. These star positions were placed on hemispheres and made into star atlases. Plancius actually proposed nine new constellations, with only three still recognized today. The Camelopardalis constellation is in the northern

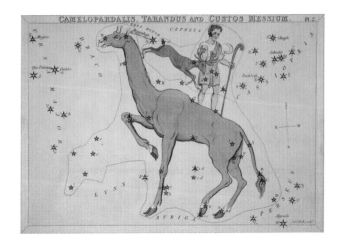

hemisphere and is visible all year round from mid-northern latitudes, with its head near the celestial pole. No one seems to know why this particular arrangement was used, but it may have had some religious significance. The German astronomer Jakob Bartsch included Camelopardalis on his star map of 1624 and wrote that it represented the camel on which Rebecca rode into Canaan for her marriage to Isaac, the son of Abraham (Genesis 24:26). This misnomer may have arisen due to the fact that the old Dutch for giraffe was *kamel*.

By the seventeenth century the giraffe began to be painted in perfect anatomical proportions; the royal French and British giraffes of the 1820s appear as great portrait paintings and were created not just for zoological purposes but as works of art for their royal owners and for the general public to admire. In Nicolas Hüet's portrait we see the Parisian giraffe standing under a pine tree, with its Arab keeper with his back to the artist, while the *Nubian Giraffe* by Jacques-Laurent Agasse (*c.* 1827, p. 83) shows the British giraffe in Windsor park with its Arab

'Camelopardalis giraffa – the giraffe'; lithograph after a drawing by Captain Thomas Brown, in *The Edinburgh Journal of Natural History and of the Physical Sciences*, vol. I (1835–9).

keeper. In the background are the Egyptian cows which were used to supply the young giraffe with milk.

It was not until the mid-nineteenth century that the giraffe began to be depicted in its natural arid environment. Great herds of giraffe were still extant in Africa at this time, and hunting game was the vogue for the richer Europeans. Art from this time is often morbid and dramatic, popular subjects illustrating

One of Salvador Dalí's most famous 'burning giraffe' works, *Burning Giraffes in Brown* from 1972.

the giraffe hunt, the chase or the kill. Few artists chose to show the captive giraffe.

As art and the artist moved away from the naturalistic to the abstract and symbolic, so did images of the giraffe. Salvador Dalí, the surrealist Spanish painter who included the giraffe in many of his works, provides a striking example. Most of the giraffes are depicted in various states of conflagration, with their manes ablaze. Oddly enough, the flaming giraffe image was first used by Dalí in his 1930 film *L'Âge d'Or* (*The Golden Age*). However, in his artwork it was not until 1937 that the first images appeared; the most well known of these are *The Burning Giraffe* and *The Invention of Monsters*. In the background of both works there is a single giraffe with its mane on fire.

The *Invention of Monsters* painting was inspired by the war in Europe looming on the horizon; as Dalí said 'According to

Nostradamus the apparition of monsters presages the outbreak of war' adding that 'the flaming giraffe equals masculine cosmic apocalyptic monster'. To Dalí the giraffe symbolizes masculinity; some commentators go further and suggest that the neck represents the phallus. At least three other works from this year repeated this motif: two charcoal sketches titled *Dinner in the Desert Lighted by Giraffes on Fire* and another sketch, *Burning Giraffe*. A decade later Dalí produced *L'elephante giraffe* (1948), which is more elephantine then giraffe and notable for not having any flames. Another decade later and the flaming giraffe reappears; in *Burning Giraffes and Telephones* (1957) three flaming giraffes are in the background. The link to telephones is hard to see. A sketch from 1970 called the *Surrealistic Bullfight, The Giraffe on Fire*, shows Dalí's most realistic giraffine image, but this time the giraffe seems to have been partially consumed by the flames instead of having a burning mane.

In a 1971 series of paintings representing professions, a rather thin-looking giraffe appears in the background of the *entrepreneurs* painting. *The Giraffes of Avignon* or *Burning Giraffes in Brown* (1975) features an impressive array of nine blazing giraffes set in two rows of four, with one taller central giraffe at the back, its mane blazing red fire instead of the standard orange, while in the foreground, a father shows them to a child. The *Saturnian Giraffe* (1974), my favourite, depicts a white giraffe that has a smouldering neck with smoke filling the bright ultramarine sky behind; this theme is repeated with a blue flaming giraffe in the Le Jungle Humaine series of 1976. Finally, as a bizarre twist, the work *Burning Giraffes in Yellow* (1982) shows a pastoral scene of a baby and Madonna figure but without a single giraffe in sight, ablaze or otherwise.

Dalí clearly used giraffe symbolism in his art throughout his career but whether he ever saw one in the wild or a zoo is not

The preserved body of a 3-metre-high female giraffe forms the centrepiece of Dr Gunther von Hagens' *BodyWorlds* exhibition in London, 2008.

known. Pablo Picasso, a contemporary of Dalí, said of the giraffe: 'God is really only another artist. He invented the giraffe, the elephant, and the cat. He has no real style. He just keeps on trying other things.'

The giraffe still provides an instantly recognizable image of the natural world to this day. The *BodyWorlds* show by the controversial German anatomist Gunther von Hagens includes a 'plasticized' four-metre tall giraffe, dissected to show its heart and muscles. The giraffe, which usually takes central stage, took three years to complete, ten times longer than the amount of time it takes to prepare a human body. Ten people are required to move the giraffe because of its weight.

Today the image of the giraffe surrounds us all, and if you go into any greeting-card retailers you are certain to find images of

Anonymous American watercolour painting of a giraffe, 1936.

A 1980s French crystal and enamel giraffe head.

Batik design
of giraffes
with a gazelle.

it, from cute photographs of a mother giraffe nuzzling her calf, to cartoon giraffes of all shapes, patterns and colours. In the wrapping-paper section you may find a paper patterned like a giraffe's coat, or a Noah's Ark motif, while next to this you often find giraffe-shaped pens, pencils and bookmarks. The poster section will also contain many images of the giraffe. Giraffe-skin prints adorn many fabrics, furnishings, clothes, handbags and shoes, and always seems to be in fashion.

The association of the giraffe with the newly born baby is a new phenomenon and like the teddy bear it is now to be found adorning baby clothes and paraphernalia, with a toy giraffe seemingly owned by every baby born in the civilized world. A French soft-rubber toy giraffe, 'Sophie', has been a favourite for babies since 1961; the manufacturers state that 'the dark contrasting pattern . . . provides visual stimulation for the baby'. Indeed a giraffe is the symbol of one of the world's largest chain of toy stores, Toys 'R' Us. Geoffrey the giraffe appears on the outside of many of its stores, and is possibly now the most famous giraffe in the world.

The giraffe is often used as a company name; the largest of these is a global chain of restaurants simply called Giraffe, founded in 1998. Throughout the world, the giraffe adorns a variety of restaurant names such as the Pink Giraffe and Blue Giraffe. The giraffe's Swahili name, twiga, is used for restaurants and a variety of companies such as Twiga Cement. In Brisbane, Australia, there a chain of coffee shops called Zarafa Coffee, a clever use of the name linking the Arabic origins of both coffee and the giraffe's name. The giraffe lends its name to a range of companies from advertising agencies to insurance companies and hotels, such as the Hotel Giraffe in Manhattan, New York. There is a Giraffe Lake in Africa and at least one Giraffe Creek, for example in Wyoming, and a recently discovered oilfield in

Embroidered sampler from 1837 depicting a 'royal' giraffe with its keeper.

Jesus, permit thy gracious Name to stand,
As the first Efforts of an Infant's hand;
And while her Fingers on the Canvass move,
Engage her tender Thoughts to seek thy Love:
With thy dear Children let her have a part,
And write thy Name thyself upon her heart.

Elizabeth Mastern
finished May 4 1837.

Uganda (the biggest ever found in sub-Saharan Africa). Throughout the past 150 years many ships have been registered with the name 'giraffe': many sailing ships from the nineteenth century and a 15,000-ton US Navy ship that served in the Second World War as an auxiliary vessel.

The giraffe is now a symbol of the modern world. It is no longer a mystical creature, but one that everyone encounters, certainly in captivity and if they are lucky in the semi-wild of an African game reserve. Today giraffe images are everywhere, utilized in every area of commercial activity. Ironically, the commercialization of the giraffe has ensured its existence; people now care about the survival of the giraffe, as the world's conservationist's agencies finally recognize that there is a need to conserve the rarest of species such as the Niger giraffe (*G.c. peralta*). Living alongside man, these so called 'white' giraffes are no longer afraid of people and will eat valuable cash crops (like cowpeas and mangoes) when food is in short supply. It is only through local tolerance and the tourist dollar that this giraffe population survives.[7]

The appearance of the giraffe in literature began in the nineteenth century, when the pioneers of Empire, particularly Europeans, first described the giraffe in the wild. The exploration and colonization of the African interior and the craze for big game hunting provided literary vehicles. One of the earliest of these books is by Lieutenant William Paterson. In his book *A Narrative of Four Journeys into the Country of the Hottentots and Caffraria* (1779), though it is principally a botanical expedition of southeastern Africa, he describes his first giraffe kill and provides a list of its dimensions. This is the giraffe that was sent to the Hunterian Museum, London and was the first ever specimen to be seen in the the the UK. In northeast Africa, in *The Nile Tributaries of Abyssinia and the Sword Hunters of the Hamran Arabs* by Sir Samuel White-Baker (1867), the author describes the joys of hunting and the associated culinary delights of the animals once shot. It is interesting to note the continuous sighting of numerous giraffes, with herds ranging from 28 to 154; sometimes they were even 'too numerous to estimate'. Likewise, H. Anderson Bryden in his book *Gun and Camera in Southern Africa* (1893) describes numerous herds of giraffe and plenty more

hunting, now using more high-powered rifles. He also reports
the thrill of drinking milk from a freshly shot nursing female.

In *In the Heart of Africa*, White-Baker describes how having
spent two hours of creeping up downwind on a herd of giraffe,
when he was just within two hundred metres the wind direction
changed, and his smell alerted the three closest giraffes to his
presence. On realizing the danger the whole herd moved off. He
gave pursuit on horseback and despite falling down a burrow
hole, he got his kill: a bull giraffe.[8]

Henry Stanley, the famous Victorian explorer, also hunted
giraffes and describes how he melted down his zinc canteens in

order to make extra hard bullets to more easily penetrate the giraffe's hide.[9] His description of one such encounter ends:

> He staggered, reeled, then made a short gallop; but the blood was spouting from the wound in a thick stream, and before he had gone 200 yards he came to a dead halt, with his ears drawn back, and allowed me to come within twenty yards of him, when receiving a zinc bullet through the head, he fell dead.

However, by the turn of the twentieth century the attitude to giraffes had changed dramatically. During this short period the giraffe population had crashed through a combination of over-hunting and disease. Based in what is now Tanzania, C. G. Schilling in his book *With Flashlight and Rifle* (1906) describes how the giraffe's demise had been driven by the trade in its hide, as it was used to make the long whips the Boer farmers used to drive their cattle. In Schilling's area the local soldiers even shot giraffe to improve their marksmanship, leaving the carcasses to rot on the ground. Despite this wanton slaughter the author had killed several large bull giraffes, as he was attempting to 'conserve' them as zoological specimens. Unfortunately, he was unable to preserve their skins as he did not have enough chemical preservatives with him when on safari. He lamented that very few European museums have large stuffed bull specimens.

> I soon saw the uselessness of my efforts and after having spoilt three skins I left the old bulls undisturbed. This was doubly hard, because I knew that soon it would be too late! No gold on earth would then be able to re-create these rare creatures.

The first fictional works appear at this time, and are principally adventure stories involving wild giraffes. In my opinion the best of these is *Giraffe Hunters* by Captain Mayne Reid (1852).[10] This book reflects the attitudes and methods of the hunters reported in the non-fictional works. *Giraffe Hunters* is a story for young adult readers, describing the adventures of three Dutch youths who plan to make their fortune by capturing and exporting a pair of live giraffes from South Africa to Europe, where the Consul of the Netherlands would pay them £500 for each animal.

Their story starts as they travel up the Limpopo River. After some minor adventures the three and their entourage discover giraffes and soon start chasing and shooting them, which seems odd behaviour if they are after live specimens. While exhibiting a 'gung-ho' attitude about hunting they also express their wonderment at the beauty of nature and the animals they kill, which include giraffes:

> Proudly the hunters dismounted by the side of the now prostrate but once stately creature – once a moving monument, erected in evidence of its Creator's wisdom, but now with its form recumbent upon the carpet of the plain, its legs kicking wildly in the agonies of death.

The local tribesmen tell them that the best way to catch giraffe is to build a V-shaped corral called a hopo. These mile-long hedged structures were constructed to entrap large game when food was in short supply.[11] All the animals in the surrounding area are herded into the corral that ends with a big deep pit, where the trapped animals are speared and killed. Disaster occurs when the hunters, accompanied by dogs and beaters, flush all the animals out of the surrounding vegetation and chase them towards

the hopo. The rush includes a small herd of elephants, buffalo, a rhinoceros and several giraffes. All the animals chased head-long into the hopo fall into the pit, where carnage ensues, and the giraffes end up dead of broken necks. To make matters worse, a six-month-old calf survives but is soon found to have a broken leg, which necessitates the poor animal being shot. The three hunters do not repeat this method of capture and later, after much adventure, capture one young giraffe by outrunning it on horseback and lassoing it around the neck, and another by trapping it at the riverside.

With their two young giraffes and a herd of cows the trio's adventure continues as they struggle to take their giraffes to Cape Town, where they finally receive their bounty. The adventurers split up and the 'camelopards became fellow-passengers of the young philosopher in his voyage to Europe'.

Victorian authors began to use the giraffe as a metaphor for height and odd shape. George Eliot mentions the giraffe in two of her novels, *Felix Holt, the Radical* (1866) and *Middlemarch* (1871–2):

> Christy himself, a square-browed, broad-shouldered masculine edition of his mother not much higher than Fred's shoulder – which made it the harder that he should be held superior – was always as simple as possible, and thought no more of Fred's disinclination to scholarship than of a giraffe's, wishing that he himself were more of the same height.

On the first page of Charles Dickens's travelogue *American Notes* (1842) he complains of his cramped cabin, in which he is to spend the next few weeks crossing the Atlantic Ocean to the USA.

> Its limited dimensions would not hold more than two enormous portmanteaus . . . which could now no more be got in at the door, not to say stowed away, than a giraffe could be persuaded or forced into a flower-pot.

Herman Melville in *Moby Dick* (1856) uses the giraffe's stature to great effect when describing one of his characters, who was six feet five, as 'erect as a giraffe'.

Sir Samuel White-Baker in *In the Heart of Africa* remarks on the giraffe's eyes and describes an Arab Sheik as strikingly handsome, his eyes were like those of a giraffe, but the sudden glance of an eagle lighted them up with a flash during the excitement of conversation which showed little of the giraffe's character.[12]

A common Victorian theme even in popular literature was violence, illustrated in Alfred, Lord Tennyson's 1850 poem *In Memoriam*,[13] a domestic elegy in which God's love for human kind is opposed to a violent female 'Nature, red in tooth and claw'.[14] This balance between peace and violence is reflected in poems about the lion, the king of the jungle, and the giraffe, with its peaceful, somewhat feminine characteristics. Contemporary accounts described that when out hunting the lion surprises the giraffe by jumping on its back and will hold on tightly while the giraffe gallops off for many miles before finally succumbing to exhaustion and its inevitable death. Whether true or an urban myth, this idea is illustrated in melodramatic style in an anonymous poem, 'The Lion and the Cameleopard', from 1827:

Heedless at the ambush'd brink,
The tall giraffe stoops down to drink;
Upon him straight the savage springs
With cruel joy: the desert rings
With clanging sound of desp'rate strife –
The prey is strong and strives for life;
Plunging oft, with frantic bound,
To shake the tyrant to the ground;
Then burst's like whirlwind, through the waste,
In hope to 'scape by headlong haste:
In vain – the spoiler on his prize
Rides proudly-tearing, as he flies
For life – for life his giant might

He strains, and pours his soul in flight:
And, mad with terror, thirst and pain,
Spurns with wild hoof and thundering plain
'tis vain – the thirsty sands are drinking
His streaming blood – his strength is sinking.
The victor's fangs are in his veins –
His flanks are streaked with sanguine stains –

A dramatic Victorian view of a pride of lions attacking a giraffe, 1860.

His panting breast in foam and gore
Is bathed: he reels – his race is o'er!
He falls – and, with convulsive throe,
Resigns his throat to the raging foe;
Who revels amidst his dying moans;
While gathering round, to pick his bones,
The vultures watch in gaunt array,
Till the proud monarch quits his prey.[15]

The same gruesome subject inspired the German poet Ferdinand Freiligrath (1810–1876), whose poem *The Lion's Ride* also ends with the demise of the giraffe.[16] Observation of the giraffe in the wild soon dispelled this scenario. Dr David Livingstone of Stanley fame states that 'no one has ever seen [lions] on the withers of a giraffe'[17] while the early twentieth-century German hunter C. G. Schilling thought it more likely that the lion would bite through the neck straight away rather than risk being thrown off the giraffe's back.[18]

Between the two world wars the way the giraffe was viewed changed. The voice of animal conservation began to be heard, and the giraffe again, as in ancient times, was seen as a thing of beauty and no longer a hunter's trophy or a museum specimen.

At this time the value of tourism was just being realized, and African craftsmen began to sell simple sculptures of big game animals like giraffes, a valuable source of income. Such a giraffe carving is central to the plot of Agatha Christie's fourth novel, *The Man in the Brown Suit* (1924). This story follows the adventures of heroine Anne Beddingfield as she becomes embroiled in a murderous plot, and decides to solve a murder herself. Following the main suspect, the man in the brown suit, from London to South Africa, she soon discovers that the murderer is after some valuable diamonds. Following the clues,

Giant cloth giraffe at the *Artists' Favourites* exhibition, ICA, London, 2003.

she recovers the diamonds, and pursues her mystery man via Cape Town and train to Rhodesia, where at a half-way stop she buys a large wooden giraffe: 'It was a colossal giraffe with an impossible neck, a mild eye and a dejected tail, it had character, it had charm.' The giraffe becomes important to the story, as the diamonds are wrapped in cotton wool and inserted in the hollowed-out interior of the giraffe, where they remain hidden for the rest of the adventure. The giraffe is casually passed around throughout the rest of the story as unwanted luggage and treated with contempt by the suspects, who are all still looking for the diamonds. The murderer is finally revealed and when finally informed that he has had the diamonds with him all along, in the travel chest of our heroine, he states 'I always did hate blinking giraffe.' Just the sort of thing a villain would say in Agatha Christie's day. Christie had herself travelled to

South Africa while accompanying her first husband on a tour of the British Empire, and she certainly visited the zoo with her nephew, but whether she saw any giraffes on these occasions is not stated. Even today the carved model giraffe is a common keepsake offered to the safari park tourist, and back home these carvings fill the shelves of fashionable 'world trade' shops on many European and North American high streets; to many the carved wooden giraffe symbolizes wild Africa.

The British poet and humorist Thomas Hood (1799–1845) was one of the earliest to write about the giraffe with a humorous slant. His four-verse poem 'Ode to the Camelopard' was partly inspired by the Royal giraffes in Windsor and Paris.

Admired by noble, and by royal tongues!
    May no pernicious wind,
Or English fog, blight thy exotic lungs!
Live on in happy peace, altho' a rarity,
Nor envy thy poor cousin's more outrageous
    Parisian popularity;
Whose very leopard-rash is grown contagious
And worn on gloves and ribbons all about,
    Alas! they'll wear him out![19]

In a more serious vein, in the poem 'Sweeney among the nightingales' by T. S. Eliot, Sweeney, the subject of the poem, appears in a zoological guise, first as an ape, then a zebra and finally a 'spotted' giraffe;

APENECK SWEENEY spreads his knees
Letting his arms hang down to laugh,
The zebra stripes along his jaw
Swelling to maculate giraffe.

A giraffe handle
on a piece
made by
South African
Ardmore Ceramics.

In the first stanza of 'Dreaming Spires' (1946) by poet Roy
Campbell (1901–1957), the author refers to giraffes as 'a People,
Who live between the earth and skies', and likens them to
steeples, 'Keeping a light-house with their eyes'. The most extensive appearance of the giraffe is in children's literature. The
novelist, essayist, journalist and biographer Hilaire Belloc
(1896–1953) included the giraffe in his best-selling children's
book, *The Bad Child's Book of Beasts* (1896). The poem begins:

The Camelopard, it is said
  By travellers (who never lie),
He cannot stretch out straight in bed
Because he is so high.

The hypochondriac giraffe Melman is shown with his screen companions from the 2008 film *Madagascar: Escape 2 Africa*.

In the *Just So Stories* (1902) by Rudyard Kipling, the giraffe features in two stories: only briefly in 'The Elephant's Child', where the giraffe is the tall uncle who ends up spanking the elephant with his 'hard, hard, hoof' after the young elephant asks him what made his skin spotty, and in a more central role in 'How the Leopard Got His Spots'. A giraffe along with a zebra and a variety of antelope, who were all at this time 'sandy-yellow-brownish all over', become tired of being hunted by the leopard and his Ethiopian companion, so they decide to move away from the savannah (high veldt) to the forest. While living in the dappled forest, the giraffe becomes blotchy and the zebra stripy. Eventually, feeling hungry, the leopard and his friend seek out

141

the giraffe and zebra in the forest. Now camouflaged, the leopard finds that 'I can smell giraffe, and I can hear giraffe, but I can't see giraffe.' Not being able to find either the giraffe or the zebra, he realizes the advantages of camouflage, and with his companion's help acquires a spotted coat, 'I'll take spots, then . . . I wouldn't look like a giraffe – not for ever so.'

The giraffe features in dozens of pre-school children's books, where it often appears either as a supporting character or a central character. Examples include *The Giraffe Who Was Afraid of Heights* by David A. Ufer and the popular *Giraffes Can't Dance* by Giles Andreae. The giraffe also features in countless 'pop-up' books, as its long neck makes it an ideal subject. Roald Dahl's *The Giraffe, the Pelly and Me* is a story about a window-cleaning giraffe. The monkey in this story mimics the monkeys depicted in Ancient Egyptian tomb art by always clinging to the giraffe's neck.

The giraffe as a modern mythical animal is central to two children's stories. In *The White Giraffe* by Peter Hallard (1969), the principal character is Martin, aged thirteen, who is dramatically separated from his parents while escaping an African bush fire. He saves himself by riding on the back of Zimbaba, the white giraffe. Eventually, after a short adventure the fire is over and Martin, Zimbaba and Martin's parents are happily reunited. In 2006 Lauren St John published her book *The White Giraffe*, the first in series of four. The author grew up in Zimbabwe and was lucky enough to have a pet giraffe of her very own. The central character of this series is Martine Allen, who at eleven years old loses her parents in a house fire and consequently moves to South Africa to live with her grandmother on a game reserve called Sawubona. The adventures start when she meets a legendary white giraffe which at first only appears at night. Martine befriends the giraffe, called Jemmy for short, and while everyone is asleep learns to ride it, having many adventures along the way. Martine and Jemmy are both special as according to Zulu legend the child that rides the white giraffe has special power over animals; a power she uses to great effect in the subsequent series of books.

The giraffe is even more popular in films and on television. It appears in several Walt Disney films. In the early cartoon *Dumbo* (1941) giraffes play a background role, forming part of the travelling menagerie; they are prominent when transported by train, with their long necks and heads sticking out of the railway carriages. In the film *The Lion King* (1994) and subsequent series, the giraffes are still only background characters and in the first film are shown paying homage to Simba's father the King. In *The Wild* (2006) a giraffe finally gets a central role; Bridgette is the only female in a group of zoo animals. Bridgette is quick-witted and wants to be seen as strong and independent. Around the same time Disney's rival DreamWorks released *Madagascar* (2005), with its captive giraffe, Melman, who is a hypochondriac. He escapes with his companions to the Indian Ocean island of Madagascar, where he meets lemurs and a host of other animals. Melman returns in 2009 in *Madagascar: Escape 2 Africa*, where we are introduced to his family. The Madagascar merchandise allows Melman to appear in all sorts of formats from a soft toy to a sneezy computer character.

The cartoon giraffe occurs in many TV programmes for pre-school children. In *64 Zoo Lane*, the main character, nine-year-old Lucy who lives next to a zoo, has a giraffe friend called Georgina.

A pair of giraffes is always a certainty when Noah's Ark is depicted. In the film *Evan Almighty* (2007) the main character, played by Steve Carell, is asked by God, played by Morgan Freeman, to build an ark for a forthcoming flood; a pair of giraffes help with the construction of the ark. In fact, only one giraffe was

A display of mounted giraffe at Montagu House, the old British Museum in London (1845). From a water-colour by George Scharf (1788–1860).

used during filming, and this giraffe, named Tweet, has starred in other films such as *Ace Ventura: Pet Detective* and a series of adverts for Toys 'R' Us. Sadly Tweet died on the set of the film *The Zookeeper* in 2009.

In modern adult literature the giraffe appears in only a handful of novels. The most well known of these is *Zarafa* by Michael Allin (1998). This fictional work was inspired by the modern revival of the story of the royal French Giraffe, Sennari, in 1984 when the Musée de L'ile de France organized an exhibition called 'Une Girafe pour Le Roi'. This exhibition proved popular and led a year later to a book of the same name by Gabriel Dardaud. This was followed by a number of children's books which describe the journey such as *The Giraffe That Walked to Paris* (1992) by Nancy Milton, The *King's Giraffe* (1996) by Peter and Mary Jo Collier, and *A Giraffe for France* (2000) by Leith

Hillard. Inspired by the success of these books, *Chee-Lin: A Giraffe's Journey* by James Rumford (2008), set in the fifteenth century, describes 'Tweega's' odyssey from East Africa via India to Peking, where he meets the Chinese Emperor.

In *The Journey of the Tall Horse: A Story of African Theatre* (2005), Mervyn Millar describes how a South African theatre company used the story of the royal French giraffe to celebrate the coming together of different cultures. The French novel *La Girafe* (1993) by Marie Nimier, translated into English by Mary Feeney as *The Giraffe*, also draws heavily on this story and fictionalizes the viewpoint of Yussef the Nubian, who looked after the giraffe on its long journey from Egypt to Paris. The main story however is focused on a disturbed youth called Joseph, who through luck is taken on as a junior zookeeper to look after a recently imported young female giraffe called Solange. After brining it back from southern France to Paris he develops a close emotional relationship with Solange. While the reader gains lots of interesting insights and facts about giraffe, the bizarre story leads to the giraffe's death mainly through Joseph's inactions. After this the tale continues with Joseph dealing with his subsequent guilt, which requires him to make daily pilgrimages to the Museum of Natural History to see and care for her skeleton.

Two biographies of people who have studied or raised giraffes are *Raising Daisy Rothschild* by Jock and Betty Leslie-Melville (made later into a 1979 TV film, *The Last Giraffe*) and *Pursuing Giraffes: A 1950s Adventure* by Anne Innis Dagg (2006). The Melvilles' story is about the capture of two young Rothschild giraffes in Kenya, first a female, Daisy, and then a male, Marlon. The calves were captured and rescued from the wild as they were thought to be under threat from poaching. The calves were caught using the pursuit and lasso technique. (Nowadays, giraffes are immobilized using a tranquilizer dart and rifle.) After keeping

the calves isolated for a few days and getting them to drink forti-
fied cow's milk from a pan, the animals soon imprinted on their
new owners, Betty and Jock. The giraffe were then transported
250 miles by minibus to their new home, the Leslie-Melvilles'
large Nairobi suburban garden. The book details their efforts
over about a year to bring up the two giraffe, which they succeed
doing with plenty of loving care, attention and carrots. The book
certainly provides a window into the psyche of the giraffe and
shows how intelligent and funny they can be.

Dagg's autobiography *Pursuing Giraffe* describes the exploits
of a newly graduated Canadian zoologist as she fulfils a lifelong
wish to study giraffes in their natural environment. Set in the
1950s, this book is unique; apart from describing the travels of
a women around Africa, it details the first modern attempt to
study a single mammal in its native habitat. Lodging on a South
African fruit farm for several months, Dagg observed and recorded the behaviour of a small group of giraffes. This work was
later published in many scientific articles and books in what
became a career for Dagg.

The book most people have come across with a giraffe in the
title is *The Tears of the Giraffe* by Alexander McCall Smith
(2000). The title itself does not refer specifically to giraffes particularly but describes the name of a traditional Botswanan
woven basket pattern. Legend states that the giraffe gave the
women their tears to weave into the basket.

'But why did the giraffe give its tears?'

Mama Ramotswe, shrugged; she had never thought
about it. ' I suppose that it means that we can all give
something,' she said. 'A giraffe has nothing else to give –
only tears' did it mean that? she wondered. And for a
moment she imagined that she saw a giraffe peering down

through the trees, its strange, stilt-borne body camouflaged among the leaves; and its moist velvet cheeks and liquid eyes.

A remarkable fictional work published recently and given a simple title is *Giraffe* (2006) by the Scottish writer J. M. Ledgard. This book is based upon a true and tragic event that happened in April 1975 in the Dvur Králové Zoo in communist Czechoslovakia. This true story would have remained hidden if it had not been for the journalistic enquiries of the author, and is still not officially recognized by the Czech government. The book begins with the birth of the giraffe Sněhurka (Snow White), who describes how she was lassoed and captured on the African plains before being shipped off to the zoo. The narration is then taken over by Emil Freymann, a physiologist whose area of expertise is haemodynamics. He is employed to accompany the captured herd of around thirty animals from Germany, where they have arrived by barge from Africa. Finally, a young factory worker Amina is introduced into the story; fascinated by giraffes, she visits the zoo as often as possible. After two years the thriving animals have increased in number to around fifty when tragedy strikes; the keeper begins to notice that the giraffes are stumbling, salivating and being lethargic. These observations finally trigger the secret night-time slaughter of the herd by two local hunters who are drafted in because of their good marksmanship. All the giraffe are destroyed by a shot to the head. The book records the slaughter of the world's largest captive giraffe herd (including many pregnant giraffes), shot simply to prevent the outbreak of a particularly virulent strain of foot and mouth disease.

Most of the adult literature about the giraffe is negative as the giraffe always ends up suffering in silence, being the hapless victim of man's wrongdoings.

The written word gives us a good description of the giraffe in its natural habitat, its quintessential features and characteristics. In children's fiction the giraffe is always a jolly character, a comical character. Often, like the story of the Ugly Duckling, it is used to illustrate how being different is something that we all get used to and should celebrate. In adult fiction the giraffe appears surprisingly rarely, and the average adult reader would find it hard to name a book featuring a giraffe. In other media such as film, again the giraffe appears in the children's realm, in many cartoons both short and long, and most children will be able to name a cartoon giraffe. In the adult arena few films feature the animal, and it is only through its biblical connections that it appears at all. This quiet and placid animal obviously does

Out in the open giraffe camouflage is ineffective against the blue skies of the Masai Mara, Kenya.

not inspire the average film director and offers little drama, although I suspect to those few directors who would like to use giraffe in their production it is the simple practical difficulties of keeping the animals in shot that puts film-makers off. With the invention of ever more impressive digital imaging the giraffe may in the future appear on the big screen only by these means, as in the 2009 film *2012*.

Today the cultural impact of the giraffe is widespread. It is an animal now recognized by all the peoples of the world, its height and long neck being its most distinctive features. To some this tall animal symbolizes clean living and foresight, while to others it imparts a sense of Africa as an exotic animal of the savannah. To some of the people of its native lands the giraffe may have had a long-held religious significance, but to the majority, although respected as a thing of beauty, it was a valuable source of food and hides. The fact that we now recognize the giraffe around the world has allowed conservationists to draw our attention to the value and needs of this animal and to tell the world that this 'tall tale' is not yet over.

Timeline of the Giraffe

25 MYA	1 million years ago	8000 BC	2000 BC
Giraffe family tree begins	The first fossils of the modern giraffe appear	Earliest known petroglyphs of giraffe	The giraffe is domesticated by the Egyptians

15th century	1613	1663	1760
Appears in art	Constellation Camelopardalis named	First giraffe seen in the wild by modern Europeans	Giraffe-hunting by Europeans begins

1897	1901	1926	1933
First giraffe arrives in Russian Zoo	The okapi discovered in Congo	First giraffe arrives in Australia	First giraffes arrive in Japan

46 BC	1022	1415	1486
The giraffe is exhibited in Rome by Julius Caesar	The Arab geographer Ibn-al-Faqih describes the giraffe	First giraffe seen in China	Giraffe reappears in Florence

1826	1836	1838	1839
Two royal giraffes are sent to Paris and London	London Zoo receives its first breeding group of giraffes	First giraffe arrives in the USA	First captive giraffe born in Europe

1937	1950s	1966	2005
Salvador Dalí paints his first 'flaming' giraffe	Giraffes protected in game reserves	Longleat Safari Park opens in the UK, allowing public to mix with giraffes	Melman appears in the animated film *Madagascar*

References

1 THE GLOBAL GIRAFFE

1 J. D. Skinner and C. T. Chimimba, *The Mammals of the Southern Africa Sub-region*, 3rd edn (Cambridge, 2005), p. 872.

2 C. A. Spinage, *The Book of the Giraffe* (London, 1968), p. 191.

3 E. H. Colbert, 'Was the Extinct Giraffe (Sivatherium) Known to the Early Sumerians?', *American Anthropologist*, XXXVIII (1936), pp. 605–8.

4 E. H. Colbert, 'A Skull and Mandible of Giraffokeryx Punjabiensis Pilgrim', *American Museum Noviates*, DCXXXII (1933), pp. 1–14.

5 C. Zhang et al., 'C4 Expression in the Central Inner Mongolia during the Latest Miocene and Early Pliocene', *Earth and Planetary Science Letters*, CCLXXXVII (2009), pp. 311–19.

6 S. L. Lindsey, M. N. Green and C. L. Bennett, *The Okapi: Mysterious Animal of Congo-Zaire* (Austin, TX, 1999), p. 132.

7 Sheer Lyn, *Tall Blondes: A Book about Giraffes* (Riverside, NJ, 1997), p. 168.

8 A. Hassanin et al., 'Mitochondrial DNA Variability in *Giraffa camelopardalis*: Consequences for Taxonomy, Phylogeography and Conservation of Giraffes in West and Central Africa', *Comptes Rendus Biologies*, CCCXXX (2007), pp. 265–74; D. M. Brown et al., 'Extensive Population Genetic Structure in the Giraffe', *BMC Biology*, V (2007), pp. 57–70.

9 J. B. Lamarck, *Zoological Philosophy: An Exposition with Regard to the Natural History of Animals*, trans. Hugh Elliot (London, 1914).

10 C. Darwin, *The Origin of Species by Means of Natural Selection*, 6th edn (London, 1872), p. 502.

11 R. E. Simmons and L. Scheepers, 'Winning by a Neck: Sexual
    Selection in the Evolution of the Giraffe', *American Naturalist*,
    CXLVIII (1996), pp. 771–86.
12 G. Mitchell, S. J. van Sittert and J. D. Skinner, 'Sexual Selection
    is Not the Origin of Long Necks in Giraffes', *Journal of Zoology*,
    CCLXXVIII (2009), pp. 1–6.
13 R. E. Simmons and R. Altwegg, 'Necks-for-Sex or Competing
    Browsers? A Critique of Ideas on the Evolution of Giraffe', *Journal
    of Zoology*, CCLXXXI (2010, in press).
14 N. Ludo Badlangana, J. W. Adams and P. R. Manger, 'The Giraffe
    (*Giraffa camelopardalis*) Cervical Vertebral Column: A Heuristic
    Example in Understanding Evolutionary Processes?', *Zoological
    Journal of the Linnean Society*, CLV (2009), pp. 736–57.

2 THE GIRAFFE INSIDE AND OUT

 1 G. Mitchell and J. D. Skinner, 'An Allometric Analysis of the
    Giraffe Cardiovascular System', *Comparative Biochemistry and
    Physiology*, A (2009).
 2 E. Brøndum et al., 'Jugular Venous Pooling During Lowering of
    the Head Affects Blood Pressure of the Anesthetized Giraffe',
    American Journal of Physiology, CCXCVII (2009), R1058–R1065.
 3 J.F.R. Paton, C. J. Dickinson and G. Mitchell, 'Harvey Cushing
    and the Regulation of Blood Pressure in Giraffe, Rat and Man:
    Introducing "Cushing Mechanism"', *Experimental Physiology*, XCIV
    (2009), pp. 11–17.
 4 G. van Dijk, 'Fainting in Animals', *Clinical Autonomic Research*,
    XIII (2003), pp. 247–55.
 5 A. N. Schiviz et al., 'Retinal Cone Topography of Artiodactyl
    Mammals: Influence of Body Height and Habitat', *Journal of
    Comparative Neurology*, DVII (2008), pp. 1336–50.
 6 A. I. Dagg and J. B. Foster, *The Giraffe: Its Biology, Behaviour and
    Ecology* (Malabar, FL, 1976).
 7 F. Bux et al., 'Organization of Chlolinergic, Putative
    Catecholaminergic and Serotonergic Nuclei in the Diencephalon,

Midbrain and Pons of Sub-adult Male Giraffes', *Journal of Chemical Neuroanatomy*, XXXIX (2010), pp. 189–203.

8 M. B. Kristal and M. Noonan, 'Note on Sleep in Captive Giraffes (*Giraffa camelopardalis reticulata*)', *South African Journal of Zoology*, XIV, p. 108.

9 W. Pérez et al., 'Gross Anatomy of the Intestine in the Giraffe (*Giraffa camelopardalis*)', *Anatomia Histologia Embryologia* (2009).

10 W. Wood and P. J. Weldon, 'The Scent of the Reticulated Giraffe (*Giraffa camelopardalis*)', *Biochemical Systematics and Ecology*, XXX (2002), pp. 913–17.

11 B. Leslie-Melville and J. Leslie-Melville, *Raising Daisy Rothschild* (London, 1977).

12 R. L. Dimond and W. Montagna, 'The Skin of Giraffe', *Anatomical Record*, CLXXXV (1976), pp. 63–76.

13 G. Mitchell and J. D. Skinner, 'Giraffe Thermoregulation: A Review', *Transactions of the Royal Society of South Africa*, LIX (2004), pp. 109–88.

14 V. A. Langman, O. S. Bamford and G.M.O. Maloiy, 'Respiration and Metabolism in the Giraffe', *Respiration Physiology*, L (1982), pp. 141–52; J. L. Patterson Jr et al., 'Cardiorespiratory Dynamics in the Ox and Giraffe with Comparative Observations on Man and other Mammals', *Annals of New York Academy of Science*, CXXVII (1967), pp. 393–413.

15 D. M. Pratt and V. H. Anderson, 'Giraffe Social Behaviour', *Journal of Natural History*, XIX (1985), pp. 771–81.

16 B. Shorrocks and D. P. Croft, 'Necks and Networks: A Preliminary Study of Population Tructure in the Reticulated Giraffe (*Giraffa camelopardalis reticula de Winston*)', *African Journal of Ecology*, XLVII (2009), pp. 1–8.

17 E. Z. Cameron and J. T. Du Toit, 'Social Influences on Vigilance Behaviour in Giraffes, *Giraffa camelopardalis*', *Animal Behaviour*, LXIX (2005), pp. 1337–44.

1 Tony Judd, 'Presumed Giraffe Petroglyphs in the Eastern Desert of Egypt: Style, Location and Nubian Comparisons', *Rock Art Research*, XXIII (2006), pp. 59–70.

2 Berthold Laufer, *The Giraffe in History and Art* (Chicago, 1928), p. 100.

3 T. Buquet, 'Pourquoi la Bible des Septante a-t-elle traduit lé zemer du Deutéronome en kamelopardalis? Réflexions sur le statut symbolique et alimentaire de la girafe', *Anthropozoologica*, XLI (2006), pp. 7–25.

4 L. Sprague de Camp, 'Xerxes' Okapi and Greek Geography', *Isis*, LIV (1963), pp. 123–5.

5 C. G. Schillings, trans. F. Whyte, *With Flashlight and Rifle: A Record of Hunting Adventures and of Studies in Wild Life in Equatorial East Africa* (London, 1906).

6 Aristotle, *The History of Animals*, Book VIII, part 28.

7 C. Zirkle, 'The Tumar or Cross Between the Horse and the Cow', *Isis*, XXXIII (1941), pp. 486–506.

8 J. Dobson, 'John Hunter's Giraffe', *Annals of the Royal College of Surgeons of England*, XXIV (1957), pp. 124–8.

9 Laufer, *The Giraffe in History and Art*, p. 100.

10 J. Stephenson, 'The Zoological Section of the Nuzhatu-l-Qulûb', *Isis*, II (1928), pp. 285–315.

11 Marco Polo and Rustichello of Pisa, *Travels of Marco Polo*, vol II, ed. Henry Yule and Henri Cordier (London, 1920).

12 S. M. Wilson, 'The Emperor's Giraffe', *Natural History*, CI (1992), p. 12.

13 E. Ringmar, 'Audience for a Giraffe: European Expansionism and the Quest for the Exotic', *Journal of World History*, XVII (2006), pp. 375–97.

14 Laufer, *The Giraffe in History and Art*, p. 100.

15 Charles D. Cuttler, 'Exotics in Post-Medieval European Art: Giraffes and Centaurs', *Artibus et Historiae*, XII/23 (1991), pp. 161–79.

16 C. A. Spinage, *The Book of the Giraffe* (London, 1968), p. 191.

17 B. Werness, *Encyclopedia of Animal Symbolism in Art* (London, 2004), p. 476.

18 Ibid.

19 L. C. Rookmaaker, 'The Observations of Robert Jacob Gordon (1743–1795) on Giraffes *(Giraffa camelopardalis)* found in Namaqualand', *SWA Scientific Society*, XXXVI (1982), pp. 71–90.

20 H. A. Bryden, *Nature and Sport in South Africa* (London, 1897), p. 314.

21 O. Goldsmith, *The Camelopard: A History of the Earth and Animated Nature* (Philadelphia, 1823), vol. III, pp. 161–3.

4 THE GIRAFFE RETURNS TO EUROPE

1 J. Dobson, 'John Hunter's Giraffe', *Annals of the Royal College of Surgeons of England*, XXIV (1957), pp. 124–8.

2 *Middlesex Journal and Evening Advertiser*, no. 833, 28 July 1774.

3 W. Paterson, *A Narrative of Four Journeys into the country of Hottentots and Caffraria in the years one thousand seven hundred and seventy-seven, eight and nine* (London, 1779), p. 175.

4 W. Moore, *The Knife Man* (London, 2005), p. 482.

5 E. H. Bostock, *Menageries, Circuses and Theatres* (repr London, 1972), p. 305.

6 O. Lagueux, 'O. Geoffroy's Giraffe: The Hagiography of a Charismatic Mammal', *Journal of the History of Biology*, XXXVI (2003), pp. 225–47.

7 E. Ringmar, 'Audience for a Giraffe: European Expansionism and the Quest for the Exotic', *Journal of World History*, XVII (2006), pp. 375–97.

8 M. Allin, *Zarafa* (London, 1998), p. 215. This book tells the story of the epic journey in detail.

9 ' The Giraffe at Paris', *The Penny Magazine*, I/38 (1832), pp. 308–9.

10 'Fashions for March 1828', *Records of the Beau Monde*, VII/39 (1828), p. 120.

11 ' Kingly Cares – The Constitution and the Giraffe', *The Examiner*, MXXXI, 29 July 1829, p. 467.

12 C. Riedl-Dorn, *Hohes Tier. Die Geschichte der ersten Giraffe im Schönbrunn* (Braumüller, 2008), p. 200.

13 'Giraffes: Zoological Notes and Anecdotes', *Bentley's Miscellany*, XXIX (1851), pp. 469–81.

14 'The Giraffe at Paris'.

15 'Giraffes: Zoological Notes and Anecdotes'.

16 Ibid.

17 'The Giraffe or Camelopard', *Saturday Magazine*, IX/268 (1836), pp. 90–92.

18 Ibid.

19 Ibid.

20 'Giraffes: Zoological Notes and Anecdotes'.

21 Ibid.

22 V. N. Kisling Jr, *Zoo and Aquarium History: Ancient Animal Collections to Zoological Gardens* (Boca Raton, FL, 2001), p. 415.

23 'Wild Beast Farms', *The Speaker*, XIX (1899), pp. 395–6.

24 G. Bolton, 'On Giraffes Generally', *Windsor Magazine*, III (1896), pp. 261–4.

25 H. A. Bryden, 'Giraffes and How to Capture Them', *Pall Mall Magazine*, II (1893), pp. 85–95.

26 C. G. Schillings, trans. F. Whyte, *With Flashlight and Rifle: A Record of Hunting Adventures and of Studies in Wild Life in Equatorial East Africa*, vol. I (London 1906).

27 H. A. Bryden, 'The Giraffe at Home', *Chambers Journal*, VIII (1891), pp. 585–8.

28 Bryden, 'Giraffes and How to Capture Them'.

29 B. Leslie-Melville and J. Leslie-Melville, *Raising Daisy Rothschild* (London, 1977).

30 John T. McCutcheon, *In Africa: Hunting Adventures in the Big Game Country* (Indianapolis, IN, 1910), chap. 14, pp. 243–5.

31 *Encyclopaedia Britannica*, 11th edn (Cambridge, 1911), XXIV, p. 1001.

32 Kisling, *Zoo and Aquarium History*, p. 415.

33 Leslie-Melville and Leslie-Melville, *Raising Daisy Rothschild*.

1 J. Fennessy, 'GiD: Development of the Giraffe Database and Species Status Report', in *Giraffa; Bi-annual Newsletter of the International Giraffe Working Group (IGWG)*, 1/2 (2007), pp. 2–6.

2 J. P. Surand, 'Giraffes of Niger, 2007 Census and Perspectives', in *Giraffa; Bi-annual Newsletter of the International Giraffe Working Group (IGWG)*. II/1 (2008), pp. 4–7.

3 J. O. Ogutu et al., 'Dynamics of Mara-Serengeti Ungulates in Relation to Land Use Changes', *Journal of Zoology*, CCLXXVIII (2009), pp. 1–14.

4 M. Damon, 'Giraffes in Europe', in *Giraffa; Bi-annual Newsletter of the International Giraffe Working Group (IGWG)*, II/1 (2008), pp. 8–14.

5 V. N. Kisling Jr, *Zoo and Aquarium History: Ancient Animal Collections to Zoological Gardens* (Boca Raton, FL, 2001), p. 415.

6 'Low Bridge and Giraffe', *Tracks: Chesapeake and Ohio Railway Magazine*, I (1957), p. 3.

7 Richard W. Flint, 'Rufus Welch: America's Pioneer Circus Showman', *Bandwagon* XIV (1970), pp. 4–11.

8 Berthold Laufer, *The Giraffe in History and Art* (Chicago, 1928).

9 A. I. Dagg and J. B. Foster, *The Giraffe: Its Biology, Behaviour and Ecology* (Malabar, FL, 1976).

10 A. Innis Dagg, *Pursuing Giraffe: A 1950s Adventure* (Waterloo, Ontario, 2006).

11 Lorenzo Hagenbeck, trans. Alec Brown, *Animals are My Life* (London, 1956), p. 293.

12 Kisling, *Zoo and Aquarium History*, p. 415.

13 Fred B. Bercovitch, Meridith J. Bashaw and Susan M. del Castillo, 'Sociosexual Behaviour, Male Mating Tactics, and the Reproductive Cycle of Giraffe *Giraffa camelopardalis*', *Hormones and Behavior*, L (2006), pp. 314–21.

14 B. Leslie-Melville and J. Leslie-Melville, *Raising Daisy Rothschild* (London, 1977)

1 Hartmann Wolfram, Jeremy Silvester and Patricia Hayes, *The Colonising Camera: Photographs in the Making of Namibian History* (Athens, OH, 1999), p. 227.

2 H. A. Bryden, *Gun and Camera in Southern Africa: A Year of Wandering in Bechuanaland, the Kalahari Desert and the River Country, Ngamiland: Notes on Colonisation, Natives, Natural History and Sport* (London, 1893), p. 544.

3 M. Danahay, 'Nature Red in Hoof and Paw: Domestic Animals and Violence in Victorian Art', in *Victorian Animal Dreams: Representation of Animals in Victorian Literature and Culture*, ed. Deborah Denenholz and Martin A. Danahay (Farnham, 2007), p. 281.

4 Elizabeth Caspari, *Animal Life in Nature, Myth and Dreams* (Chicago, 2003), p. 317; Remke Kruk, 'Elusive Giraffes: Ibn Abi LḤawāfir's Badā'I' Al-Akwān and Other Animal Books', in *Arab Painting: Text and Image in Illustrated Arabic Manuscripts*, ed. Anna Contadini (Leiden, 2007).

5 Ibid.

6 *The Travels of Sir John Mandeville* (1371).

7 R. Leroy et al., 'The Last African White Giraffes Live in Farmers' Fields', *Biodiversity and Conservation*, XVIII (2009), pp. 2663–77.

8 Samuel White-Baker, *In the Heart of Africa* (New York, 1884), p. 286.

9 Henry M. Stanley, *How I Found Livingstone* (London, 1872), p. 736.

10 Mayne Reid, *The Giraffe Hunters* (New York, 1852), p. 336.

11 David Livingstone, *Livingstone's Travels and Researches in South Africa* (Philadelphia, PA, 1859), p. 436.

12 White-Baker, *In the Heart of Africa*, p. 286.

13 Alfred Lord Tennyson, *In Memoriam AHH*, ed. W. J. Rolfe (New York, 1895).

14 Danahay, 'Nature Red in Hoof and Paw', p. 281.

15 *Lady's Monthly Museum or Polite Repository of Amusement and Instruction*, XXVI (1827), pp. 203–4.

16 *Poems by Ferdinand Freiligrath, edited by his Daughter*, Collection of German authors, vol. XIII (London, 1871), p. 260.

17 Stanley, *How I Found Livingstone*, p. 736.

18 C. G. Schillings, trans. F. Whyte, *With Flashlight and Rifle: A Record of Hunting Adventures and of Studies in Wild Life in Equatorial East Africa* (London 1906).

19 *The Works of Thomas Hood*, vol. III (New York, 1864).

Select Bibliography

Allin, M., *Zarafa* (London, 1998)

Belozerskaya, Marina. *The Medici Giraffe: And Other Tales of Exotic Animals and Power* (New York, 2006)

Bonnett, Wexo J., *Giraffes* (Poway, CA, 2001)

Bryden, H. A., *Gun and Camera in Southern Africa: A Year of Wandering in Bechuanaland, the Kalahari Desert and the River Country, Ngamiland: Notes on Colonisation, Natives, Natural History and Sport* (London, 1893)

—, *Nature and Sport in South Africa* (London, 1897)

Hagenbeck, Lorenzo, *Animals Are My Life* (London, 1956)

Innis Dagg, A., and J. B. Foster, *The Giraffe: Its Biology, Behaviour and Ecology* (Malabar, FL, 1976)

—, *Pursuing Giraffe: A 1950s Adventure* (Waterloo, Ontario, 2006)

Keevil Parker, B., *Giraffes* (Minneapolis, MN, 2004)

Kisling Jr, V. N., *Zoo and Aquarium History: Ancient Animal Collections to Zoological Gardens* (Boca Raton, FL, 2001)

Laufer, Berthold, *The Giraffe in History and Art* (Chicago, 1928)

Leslie-Melville, B., and J. Leslic Melville, *Raising Daisy Rothschild* (London, 1977)

Lindsey, S. L., M. N. Green and C. L. Bennett, *The Okapi: Mysterious Animal of Congo-Zaire* (Austin, TX, 1999)

Livingstone, David, *Livingstone's Travels and Researches in South Africa* (Philadelphia, 1859)

Paterson, W. A., *Narrative of Four Journeys into the country of Hottentots and Caffraria in the years one thousand seven hundred and seventy-seven, eight and nine* (London 1779)

Reid, Mayne, *The Giraffe Hunters* (New York, 1852)

Roosevelt T., *African Game Trails* (New York, 1910)

Schillings, C. G., *With Flashlight and Rifle: A Record of Hunting Adventures and of Studies in Wild Life in Equatorial East Africa* (London, 1906)

Sheer, Lyn, *Tall Blondes: A Book About Giraffes* (Riverside, NJ, 1997)

Spinage, C. A., *The Book of the Giraffe* (London, 1968)

Stanley, Henry M., *How I Found Livingstone* (London, 1872)

White-Baker, Samuel, *In the Heart of Africa* (New York, 1884)

Associations and Websites

The African Fund for Endangered Wildlife Kenya (AFEW Kenya Ltd), also known as the Giraffe Centre, is a charity supporting giraffe conservation in Kenya.
www.giraffecenter.org

The newsletters of the International Union for Conservation of Nature (IUCN), Species survival commission (SSC), Antelope Specialist Group (ASG) and International Giraffe Working Group (IGWG) provide information about giraffe conservation in the wild and in zoos worldwide
www.giraffeconservation.org

The American Zoo and Aquarium Association's (AZA) Antelope Taxon Advisory Group (TAG), provide information of captive giraffe numbers in zoos across North America.
www.antelopetag.com

International Association of Giraffe Care professionals
www.giraffecare.org

Association pour la Sauvegarde des giraffes du Niger.
www.asgn-association-sauvegarde-girafe-niger.html

Giraffe line clothing: a percentage of profits go to the Giraffe Conservation Foundation (GCF)
www.giraffeline.com

The Rothchild's Giraffe Project
www.girafferesearch.com

A project to get the public to upload one million giraffe images
www.onemilliongiraffes.com

Acknowledgements

The giraffe represents a lifelong personal interest. As a child I remember being impressed by its great height and strange markings, and then as a adult and graduate biologist I began to read widely about its unusual biology and its cultural history. Writing this book has allowed me to indulge in this lifelong fascination and immerse myself in everything giraffine.

It is impossible to include everything about the giraffe so I hope this selection of the giraffe's natural and social history provides a good overall view of its interaction with mankind. Whenever possible I have checked original sources, but this was not always possible.

I am indebted to the many giraffe keepers who have spoken to me at zoos around the world. The experts Marc Damen, Julian Fennessy and Lorraine Jolly deserve special mention, as they freely provided information on current giraffe numbers in the wild and in captivity.

The staff of Reaktion Books also deserve special mention, for without them this book would not have been possible. Finally, I would like to dedicate this book to Karen and Laura, for without their enduring love, support and encouragement this work would never have been completed.

Photo Acknowledgements

The author and publishers wish to express their thanks to the below sources of illustrative material and/or permission to reproduce it. (Some sources uncredited in the captions for reasons of brevity are also given below.)

Photo Action Press/Rex Features: p. 114; Art Institute of Chicago (gift of Mrs Robert B. Mayer, photo © The Art Institute of Chicago): p. 53; from Jehoshaphat Aspin, *A Familiar Treatise on Astronomy* . . . (London, 1825): p. 120; photos author: pp. 25, 105; photo Chris Martin Bahr/Rex Features: p. 12; Bibliotheca Apostolica Vaticana, Vatican City, Rome: p. 59; Bibliothèque Centrale du Museum National d'Histoire Naturelle, Paris: pp. 80, 82; licensee BioMed Central Ltd.: p. 13; Bodleian Library, Oxford (Manuscripts and Early Printed Books): p. 63; courtesy of the Bradshaw Foundation: p. 46; from Carel Frederik Brink, *Nouvelle description du Cap de Bonne-Espérance avec un journal historique d'un voyage de terre* . . . (Amsterdam, 1778): p. 67; British Library, London: p. 92; British Museum, London (photos © Trustees of the British Museum): pp. 47 (bottom left), 62, 65, 68, 133, 147; photo © The Trustees of the British Museum: p. 84; photo John Paul Brooke/Rex Features: p. 113; from David M. Brown et al., 'Extensive Population Genetic Structure in the Giraffe' in *BMC Biology* 5:57 (2007), at http://www.biomedcentral.com/1741-7007/5/57 © 2007 Brown et al.: p. 13; from the Comte de Buffon, *Histoire Naturelle, Générale et Particulière* . . . : pp. 67 left [vol. III (Paris, 1750 edition)], 70 [vol. XIII (Paris, 1752 edition)]; photo John Curtis/Rex Features: p. 104; from *The Edinburgh Journal of Natural History and of the Physical Sciences*, vol. I (1835–39): p. 121; photo F1 Online/Rex Features: p. 39; photo Fotex Medien Agentur GMBH/Rex Features: p. 23; Fundação Ricardo do Espírito Santo Silva, Lisbon: p. 66; photo Gallo Images/ Getty Images: pp. 26, 30; from Captain W. Cornwallis Harris, *Portraits of the Game and Wild Animals of Southern Africa, Delineated from Life in their Native Haunts . . .* (London, 1840): p. 73; photo ITV/Rex Features: p. 112; photo Nils Jorgensen/Rex Features: pp. 124, 140; Library of Congress, Washington, DC (Prints and Photographs Division): pp. 98, 120; illustration by Michael Long: p. 8; photo James D. Morgan/Rex Features: pp. 29, 41; Musée de l'Ile-de-France, Sceaux: p. 130; Musée du Louvre, Paris/Giraudon/The Bridgeman Art Library: p. 47 (bottom right); Museum of Fine Arts, Boston: p. 125 (top); National Gallery of Canada, Ottawa: p. 61; courtesy Natural History Museum, London: pp. 8, 144; photo Nature Picture Library/Rex Features: p. 11; photo Newspix/ Rex Features: p. 107; photo Novastock/Rex Features: p. 151; Palazzo Vecchio (Palazzo della Signoria) Florence/The Bridgeman Art Library: p. 60; photo © Paramount/Everett/Rex Features: p. 141; photo Constan-tinosPetrinos/Nature Picture Library/Rex Features: p. 28; Philadelphia Museum of Art (gift of John T. Dorrance, 1977): p. 57; private collection: p. 126; private collection/DaTo Images/Bridgeman Art Library: p. 111; from *The Prize Natural History*, by R. Lydekker and others (London, 1897): p. 117; photos Rex Features: pp. 106, 149; photo Gary Roberts/ Rex Features: pp. 6, 32; Royal Collection, © 2010, Her Majesty Queen Elizabeth II: p. 83; photo Sipa Press/Rex Features: p. 22; photo Gary M. Stolz/U.S. Fish and Wildlife Service (Division of Public Affairs): p. 20; photo Ray Tang/Rex Features: p. 138; photo Taxi/Getty Images: p. 43; from Edward Topsell, *Historie of Foure-footed Beastes* [. . .] *collected out of all the volumes of C. Gesner, and all other Writers to this present day* (London, 1607): p. 64 (foot); photo Steve & Ann Toon/Robert Harding /Rex Features: p. 32; photos Wellcome Library, London: pp. 69, 91; photos Werner Forman Archive: pp. 47 (top), 48; photoWestEnd61/ Rex Features: p. 102; photos Carol Moen Wing: pp. 14, 100; photos Jereld Wing: pp. 17, 35; Worcester Porcelain Museum: pp. 74, 86; photos © Zoological Society of London: pp. 64 (foot), 70, 73, 121.

Index

Adoration of the Magi
  (Ghirlandaio) 61, 118
Agasse, Jacques-Laurent 120
Albertus Magnus 58
Arabian 54–6, 77, 116–17
Aristotle 50
art *126, 128, 138, 147*
Australia 103, 127

Bacchiacca, Francesco 62
barn, giraffe 105–8
Bartsch, Jakob 120
Bäuerle, Adolf 87
Bellini, Gentile 62
Belloc, Hilaire 140
Belon, Pierre 66
Bewick, Thomas 71
Bible 49, 50, 118–19
Bicarlo, John 58
Bosch, Hieronymous 63
Breydenbach, Bernhard von
  62
Brink, Carel Frederik 67
Bryden, H. Anderson 94, 129
Buffon, Comte de 67–8, *67, 70*

Burton, Decimus 106
Burning Giraffes in Brown (Dalí)
  122

camel 8, 19–20, 36, 49–52, 54–5,
  66, 73, 75–6, *85*, 89, 113,
  118–20
camelopard 71, *74,* 74–5, 81, *85,*
  92, 95, 134–5, 139, 141
Camelopardalis (constellation)
  119–20, *120*
Canthumeryx sirtense 9
Campbell, Roy 140
Canada 110, 146
Charles X of France 76, *76*
China 56–8, *57,* 145
Christie, Agatha 137–9
circus, circuses 52, 92, *95,* 109–13,
  111
Clive, Lord (Clive of India) 74
Commodus, Emperor of Rome
  53–4
Constantine XI, Emperor 57
Constantinople 54, 58, 62, 87–8
Cornwallis, Captain Harris W. *73*

Cosimo, Piero di 62
Czechoslovakia 147

D'Ancona, Cyriacus *63*, *63*
Dagg, Anne Innis 145, 146
Dahl, Roald 142
Dalí, Salvador 122–3, *122*
Darwin, Charles 15–16, 18, 20
Dickens, Charles 134
dragons 57, 95

East Africa 50, 54, 55, 89, 96–7,
    99–100, 102
Egypt, Egyptians 45–9, *47–8*, 54,
    55, 58, 62, 76, 77, 82, 89, 104,
    142
Eliot, George 75, 134
Eliot, T. S. 139
elephants 55

Florence 58–61, 62
Franz II, Holy Roman Emperor
    86
Frederick II of Sicily 58
Freiligrath, Ferdinand 137

Garden of Eden 118
Gathering of Manna (Bacchiacca)
    62
George IV, King of Britain 82–6,
    83, *84*, *85*, 120
General History of Quadrupeds
    (Bewick) 71
Germany 103
Gesner, Conrad 65

Ghirlandaio, Domenico 61, 119
Giraffa jumae 10
giraffe (*Giraffa camelopardalis*)
    49, 50, 101, *121*, *125*, *151*
    behaviour 22, 28, 31, *32*, 32,
    35, 37, 42–3, *105*, 130, 146
    breeding 38–40, 50–51, 102–3
    calves *39*, 40–42, *41*, 43, 55,
    67, *94*, 96, 107, 110, *114*, 145–6
    cardiovascular system 21–5,
    32
    defence 36, 40, 96
    diet 21, 26, 31, 60, 78, 83, 86,
    94, 96, 121, 122
    drinking *23*, 24, 31, 33, 73
    eyes *25*, 25–6, 116, 146–7
    feeding 26, 33–4, 38, 55, *100*,
    108–9, 146
    fossil 7–10, 19
    lips 18, 27
    movement 25, 35–6, *35*, 48,
    97
    neck 10, *14*, 15–20, 21, 24, 29,
    29, 31, 32–3, 38, 44, 48, 55, 56,
    61, 94, 110
    neck sparring *17*, 18, 42
    ossicones 27–8, *28*, 66, 68, *70*
    parasites 31–2, 69, 97
    predators 38, 40, *136*
    respiration 35
    smell 34
    skin 34, 46, 56, 63, 67–9, 93,
    95, 99, 127, *133*, *149*
    tail 29, 36–7, *37*, 44, 49, 99
    tongue 18, *26*, 27, 29, 44

giraffe classification 12–13, *13*, 102–3
  Angolan (*G. c. angolensis*) 13, 103
  Maasai (*G. c. tippelskirchi*) 12–13, 103
  Northern (*G. c*) 7
  Reticulated (*G. c. reticulate*) 12–13, *20*
  Rothschild's or Baringo (*G. c. rothschildi*) 12–14, 103
  South African (*G. c. giraffa*) 13
  Thornicroft's (*G. c. thronicrofti*) 12–13
  Western or Nigerian (*G. c. peralta*) 7, 12–14, 101, 129
'giraffernalia' 81, *81*, 82, 87, *125*, 130, 140
Giraffe Manor, Nairobi *113*, 115
Giraffidae 7–8, 19
Giraffokeryx 9
Giulio Romano 118
Gordianus III, Emperor of Rome 53
Gordon, Robert Jacob 69–70
Greeks 49–52

Hagenbeck, Carl 103, 110
Hagenbeck, Lorenzo 111–12
Hallard, Peter 142
Hatsheput, Queen of Egypt 49
Home, Sir Everard 86
Hood, Thomas 139
Hop, Hendrik 67
Hopo 132

Hüet the Younger, Nicolas *80*, 120
Hunter, John 68, 72-73, 129
hunting (giraffe) 36, 67, *69*, 69, 89–90, 96–8, 129–31

Ibbetson, J. C. 69
India 56, 74, 103–4

Japan 111–12
Julius Caesar 52
Justin II, Emperor of Rome 58
Just So Stories 141

keeper (zoo) *60*, *77*, 79, 82, 87–8, 90, 102–3, 118, 120, *128*, 144–5, 148
Kiffian people 45
K'i-lin 56
  Kirin (Japanese) 112
Kipling, Rudyard 141

Lamarck, Jean-Baptiste 15, 20
Ledgard, J. M. 147–8
Leslie-Melville, Betty and Jock 115, 145
Le Valliant, François 68
lion 55, *117*, 135, *136*, 137
llama 19–20, 113
Ligozzi, Jacopo 118
Livingstone, David 137
Luini, Bernardino 118

McCall Smith, Alexander 146
McCutcheon, J. 97

Medici, Lorenzo de 58–61, *59*, *64*, 118
Mehmet Ali, Pasha of Egypt 75, 86
Melville, Herman 134
Melman (*Madagascar*) *141*, 143
Mother Nature 116, *117*, 135
museums 69, *69*, 73, 78, 82, 96, 110, 116, 129, 131, 137, *144*, 144, 145

New Zealand 103
Niger 45
Nimier Marie
Noah's Ark 118, 127, 143
Norway 105

okapi 9, *11*, 11, 18-19, 50, 107
Origin of Species, The 15
oxpeckers *30*, 31

Paris 69, 78–81, *80*, 120, 144, 145
Paterson, William 68, *73*, 129
Persia 50, 54, 117
petroglyphs 45, *46*,
phoenix 54, 57
Picasso, Pablo 124
Plancius, Petrus 119
Polo, Marco 55
Ponsonby, Sir F. 82
porcelain *74*, *86*

Qaitbay, al-Ashraf, Sultan of Egypt 58

Reid, Captain Mayne 132
rhinoceros 53, 133
rock art 45
Romans 50–54, *53*
Roosevelt, Theodore 96
Russia 103, 105

safari parks 113, 115
Saint-Hiliare, Étienne Geoffroy 78–9
Scharf, George *144*
Schilling, C. G. 94, 131, 137
Sivatherium 8, 9
South Africa 66, 68–70, 72, 94, 104, 132–4, 146
St John, Lauren 142
St Mark Preaching in Alexandria, Egypt (Bellini) 62
Stanley, Henry 130–31, 137
Stoer, Niklas *64*
Sumerians 9

Tennyson, Alfred Lord 135
Tookey, J. *69*
Topsell, Edward *64*
Tournai tapestry *66*
Travels of Sir John Mandeville 117
Turks 58–9, 87–8
twiga 71, 99, 127

unicorn 54, 56, 95
USA 109–10, 127

Vespucci, Amerigo 61
Victoria, Queen of England 93

Vienna 86
Von Hagens, Gunther 124–5
Vulcan and Aeolus (Piero di
    Cosimo) *61*, 62

Webber, J. *68*
White-Baker, Sir Samuel 129–30,
    134
Wombwell, G. 74–5, 92
World War II 98, 107, 128

Xerxes 50

Zarafa 49, 65, 127, 144
Zheng He 56
Zoological Society of London
    89–90, 106
zoo, zoos 49, 79–80, 90–94, *91*,
    92, *98*, 98–9, *102*, 103–4, *104*,
    105, 108, *114*, 147